DATE DUE

The Definition of Good

THE DEFINITION
OF GOOD

By

A. C. EWING

M.A., D.Phil. (Oxon); M.A., Litt.D. (Cantab).
Fellow of the British Academy
Lecturer in Moral Science in the University of Cambridge

HYPERION PRESS, INC.
Westport, Connecticut

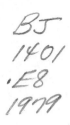

Published in 1947 by The Macmillan Co., New York
Copyright, 1947, by the Macmillan Company
Hyperion reprint edition 1979 1987
Library of Congress Catalog Number 78-59021
ISBN 0-88355-695-2
Printed in the United States of America

Library of Congress Cataloging in Publication Data
Ewing, Alfred Cyril, 1899-
    The definition of good.

    Reprint of the ed. published by Macmillan, New York.
    Includes index.
    1. Good and evil.   I. Title.
BJ1401.E8   1979   179'.9   78-59021
ISBN 0-88355-695-2

Preface

The question *What is the definition of goodness* must be distinguished from the question *What things are good;* and it is the former, not the latter, question which I discuss in this book. This question, while less immediately and obviously practical, is more fundamental, since it raises the issue whether ethics is explicable wholly in terms of something else, for example, human psychology, and it certainly ought to be answered before we decide either on the place value is to occupy in our conception of reality or on the ultimate characteristics which make one action right and another wrong.

I shall not attempt to give a list of those to whom I am indebted, because such a list would probably embrace all the main works on ethics which I have read and most of the people who have discussed with me, orally, the fundamental concepts of ethics. I must express my gratitude to my mother for her valued help in proofreading. I also have to thank the editors of *Mind* and *Philosophy* for having allowed me to use articles I had previously published in these periodicals.

A. C. EWING

TRINITY HALL
  CAMBRIDGE
  ENGLAND

November, 1946

Contents

CHAPTER I

Subjectivism

One class of answer to the question how "good" is to be defined is given by the subjectivists. But, before we consider this type of answer, we must try to make clear to ourselves what could be meant by the "objectivity" of ethical judgements or of value judgements in general. It obviously does not mean that they ascribe value properties to physical objects. These clearly do not possess ethical qualities. It might indeed be held that they possessed the property of beauty and therefore the property of intrinsic goodness quite independently of being perceived. This view does not seem to me obviously false, but it is plain that most philosophers who have asserted the objectivity of value judgements did not wish to commit themselves to it, still less to maintain that all value judgements were objective in precisely the same sense as that in which judgements about physical objects are. We can therefore rule out at once the sense of "objective" as referring to what exists independently of being experienced. What then does "objective" mean when used in reference to ethics?

1. It may mean "claiming to be true." Obviously in this sense judgements about psychological events and dispositions are objective, though they do not refer to what exists independently of experience, and in this sense ethical judgements may be objective. To say they are is indeed to say no more than that they are judgements and not merely something else which we have confused with judgements. But even this much is denied by some who maintain that so-called ethical judgements are only exclamations, commands, or wishes.

2. However, a person who admitted the occurrence of ethical judgements, but denied that they were ever in fact true or that we could ever have any justification for believing them to be true, would not usually be described as holding an objective view of ethics. So "objective" here may be taken as implying that ethical judgements in particular and value judgements in general are sometimes true and can be sometimes known or at least justifiably believed to be true. An objective view involves the rejection of scepticism in ethics.

3. But this would not by itself be sufficient to satisfy the holders of the view that ethical judgements are objective. Suppose "A is good" simply meant "I have a certain feeling about A." It would then be a judgement and could perfectly well be true and known to be true, yet anybody who maintained such a position would be said to be holding a subjective and not an objective view of ethics. The proposition that ethical judgements are objective, therefore, besides asserting that they are judgements, asserts of them a certain independence of the feelings or attitude of the person judging. They are not merely judgements about his feelings, or for that matter his thoughts. Even if partly based on feeling, they are not about the feeling itself but about something to which the feeling points, and something which cannot adequately be described in terms merely of the man's own psychology.

The view that "ethical judgements are objective" therefore excludes the following views: (a) that they are not really judgements at all, (b) that they are all false or that we are never justified in thinking them true, (c) that they are merely judgements about one's own psychological state or dispositions. Any of these three alternative views may be called "subjective."[1] The "objective" view is also commonly understood as excluding any view which holds them to be analysable

---

[1] My use of this term is quite different from the use made of it by Ross in *Foundations of Ethics*, Chap. 7.

exclusively in terms of human psychology, but here a distinction is required between "naturalism" and "subjectivism." A person who opposes naturalist theories of ethics in general is often spoken of rather loosely as defending the objectivity of ethics, but a naturalist theory need not be, though it may be, subjective.[2] A typical example of naturalist ethics would be the theory that to say some action is right or some experience good merely means that most men, or most men in a certain group, tend to have a particular kind of feeling about it or that it tends to the satisfaction of most men's desires. Now on such a theory "good" and "right" still stand for objective facts quite independent of the attitude towards them of the person who makes the ethical judgement in question; that is, they stand for facts about a class of people, or people in general. They would still be as objective as the judgement that many Germans admired Hitler or that generally a man is distressed by the death of his parents. These forms of naturalist ethics differ from non-naturalist forms not in denying the objectivity of ethics, for judgements of psychology are objective, but in making ethics a branch of an empirical science, and will therefore be discussed not in the present chapter but in the following one.

Perhaps the most striking feature of present-day ethics is the frequent occurrence of theories of a frankly naturalist or subjectivist type. For this there are several obvious causes. Firstly, the success of the natural sciences as compared with philosophy and the failure of obscurantist opposition in the name of religion have made people reluctant to admit anything which cannot be subjected to the methods of empirical science. Secondly, the decline in the influence of organized Christianity and the widespread doubts as to the justification of its central

---

[2] Of the three types of subjective theory above I should call (c) both naturalist and subjective; (a) and (b) could not claim that ethical propositions are part of a natural science, and therefore I should hesitate to call them naturalist.

theological beliefs have contributed to the rise of scepticism
about ethics. This must specially be the case with those who
thought that ethics was essentially bound up with religion but
have lost their faith in religion. Thirdly, the radical divergence in ethical views between different people and different
civilizations has been realized as never before (and, I think,
exaggerated). Fourthly, since the war of 1914–18 there has
been a world-wide reaction against rationalism in all spheres,
so that there is a consequent tendency to regard any *a priori*
element in ethics with great suspicion and to connect "value
judgements" closely with feeling, even sometimes to the extent
of saying that they are not judgements at all but only expressions of feeling. We must not, however, exaggerate the
prevalence of such opinions. When I reviewed the ethical
literature published in 1937 and 1938 in order to write a
manual for the *Institut International de Collaboration Philo-
sophique* ³ I found that on the continent of Europe naturalist
or subjectivist ethics was decidedly the exception among
philosophers. I even noted an assertion in an article by Professor Urban ⁴ that the objectivity of value can now be regarded as one of the things "we know" in axiology, in the
sense that among critical opinion there is a large measure of
assent on this point even in America and more markedly in
Europe. It is too early to say how the situation will be affected
by the war.

   The simplest form of the subjectivist view is that according
to which ethical judgements, though genuine judgements,
assert only that the person who makes the judgement has or
tends to have certain feelings. "This is good" or "right" on
such a view becomes "I have [or tend to have] an emotion of
approval on considering this." A number of incredibly para-

---

   ³ This was unfortunately never published, owing to the German occupa-
tion of Paris.
   ⁴ *Journal of Philosophy*, 1937, p. 588 ff.

doxical consequences would follow from the adoption of this view. Firstly, the judgements could not be false unless the person judging had made a mistake about his own psychology. Secondly, two different people would never mean the same thing when they made such a judgement, since each would mean "This is approved by *me*." Indeed the same person would never mean the same by it on two different occasions, because each time he would mean "I *now* feel [or tend to feel] approval of this."

Thirdly, if I judge something to be good and you judge it to be bad, our judgements would never be logically incompatible with each other. It is not a sufficient reply to point out that they can still be incompatible with each other in some different sense, for example in the sense that they express attitudes which are in conflict with each other or lead to incompatible policies. For we do not see merely that A's judgement "This is good" and B's judgement "This is bad" (in the corresponding sense of the word) lead to or express incompatible policies like A's judgement "I desire to further X" and B's judgement "I desire to oppose X." We see that the two judgements logically contradict each other so that it is logically impossible that they could both be true. No doubt, since "good" and "bad" can each be used in different senses, "this is bad" may not always contradict "this is good," because, for example, "good" may mean "instrumentally good" and "bad" may mean "intrinsically bad"; but at any rate they sometimes do so, and on the view under discussion they could, when asserted by different people, never do so. Fourthly, no argument or rational discussion, nor indeed any citation of empirical facts, could be in any degree relevant to supporting or casting doubt on any ethical judgement unless it could be directed to showing that the person who makes the judgement has made a mistake about his own feelings or tendencies to have feelings. It is true that argument or fresh knowledge about the circumstances and likely consequences of an act might lead me to have different feelings about it and so judge it right while I had judged it wrong before, or vice versa; but it would not in any way indicate that my previous judgement was false.[5] The judgements would be different; but since they referred only to my feelings at different times they would not contradict each other any more than "I was ill on January 1" contradicts "I was well on February 1." Yet it is clear that argument can really cast doubt on propositions in ethics.

Fifthly, I could not, while asserting an ethical belief, conceive that I might possibly be wrong in this belief and yet be certain that I now feel (or tend to feel) disapproval. Since it is quite clear that I can conceive this in some cases at least, this argument provides another *reductio ad absurdum* of the theory. To think that an ethical belief now expressed by me may possibly be wrong is not the same as thinking that I may come in the future to have different feelings, for I think that the present judgement may be wrong and not a future one. To put the objection in another way, it would follow from the theory that to say "If I feel approval of A, A is always right [good]" is to utter a tautology. But it is not, it is a piece of gross conceit, if made in any ordinary context. Even if it were true that, if I feel approval of A, I shall always at the time judge A to be right (good), this is quite a different statement. I need not always be certain that my judgements are correct (unless judgement is so defined as to cover only cases of *knowledge*).

---

[5] I am therefore quite unmoved by the elaborate discussion by C. L. Stevenson in *Ethics and Language* as to how argument can be relevant to ethical disagreements on a subjectivist view. It does not show it to be relevant in the sense in which we really see it to be relevant, but in some other sense. The book is no doubt a very able exposition of subjectivism for those who are already convinced, but it does not, as far as I can see, bring any real argument for it or avoid any of the objections that I have mentioned against it.

Sixthly, it would follow from the theory under discussion that, when I judge that Hitler was bad or acted wrongly, I am not really talking about Hitler at all but about my own psychology.

To me the consequences that I have mentioned are all quite incredible and constitute a fully sufficient *reductio ad absurdum* of the theory from which they are deduced. They hold whether it is applied both to "good" and to "right" or only to one of them. I do not, however, see how the theory could be applied to "right" without being also applied to "good"; but it might be held that it applied only to "good" and that "right" was to be defined as "a means to the state of affairs for which (of those producible in the context) I felt, at the time I made the judgement, most approval on the whole." This would be a naturalist non-subjectivist theory of "right" combined with a subjectivist theory of "good." However, it is clear that this cannot be the meaning of "right," for if my emotions were ill adjusted a quite wrong action might be, and be believed by me to be, the most effective means to the state of affairs for which I felt most approval. I should probably in that case not judge it to be wrong at the time (though I might even do this if I distinguished between what I really thought good and my emotional feeling of approval); but I might quite well judge afterwards not only that it was wrong but that my earlier judgement that it was right was mistaken, while admitting that the act was the most effective means to the state towards which at the time I made the first judgement I felt most approval. Nor can we define a right act as "means, etc., to the state of affairs towards which I should always or ultimately feel most approval," for that would make it a prophecy about my future emotions. It clearly would not necessarily invalidate my present judgement that some particular act is right if it should turn out that my emotional disposition changed later in my life in such a way that I no longer felt approval of the state of affairs to which the action was an efficient means. It is true that I should in that case be disposed later to contradict my present judgement, but it certainly would not mean that my present judgement as to the rightness of the act was necessarily false.

Finally, if I ask somebody for advice on a question of practical ethics, I do not merely want to be brought into a certain emotional state about the proposed act or be persuaded that it is the best means to what will produce such an emotional state in me (or in other people, for that matter). Or at least, if that is all I want (which I suppose is the case with some people's requests for advice), it would be agreed that I am not asking in the right spirit, that is, I do not really want to know what is right but only to feel comfortable about the act advised. When I am asking for ethical advice I am asking, if I am genuine, whether a proposed act has an objective characteristic and not merely about its relation to my own emotions. And likewise when I am making up my own mind I do not regard my feeling of approval as a proof, even for myself, that a certain act is right but only as an indication. Because emotions are conservative, a man may easily have the feeling of disapproval towards something he thinks right if he formerly thought it wrong or towards something which offends his taste but which he believes is ethically neutral. But there are cases where I clearly see that something is good or bad, right and obligatory or wrong, and this insight has often been confused with the feeling which usually accompanies it.

Practically the same objections apply whether the subjectivist takes ethical judgements to be about the speaker's feelings or about his thought or about an attitude of mind including feeling, thought, and conation alike. Further, if we introduce the notion of thinking into the definition, an additional objection arises. For, if "this is good or right" means or includes in its meaning "I think it good or right," it may be objected that "I think this good or right" would become "I think that I think it good or right," so that we have either a vicious circle or an infinite regress.

It should however be noted that I have not included in the objections the argument sometimes used that from the subjectivist view it would follow that the same act may be both right when I speak about it, that is, approved by me, and wrong when you speak about it, that is, disapproved by you. For on any view the same act might be both right and not right (wrong) in different senses of "right." Even on the subjectivist view it need not be both right and not right in the same sense of "right." It is, however, very hard to believe that "good" or "right" means something different every time the word is used by a different speaker, and this is a furthur objection.

We should note an ambiguity in the terms "approval" and "disapproval." As used in recent philosophical discussion they have commonly stood for emotions, but in ordinary speech they usually express a judgement. "I approve of A" is then identical with "I judge A good," "I disapprove of A" with "I judge A bad" (in some respect at least). All ethical judgements express approval or disapproval in this sense, as all judgements without exception express the thoughts of the person who makes them. But if I therefore went on to say that I meant by "A is good" that I approve of A, I should be saying that I meant by "A is good" that I judge that A is good. This as a definition is obviously circular.

None of the objections I have given are avoided by substituting for "feelings" "tendencies to have feelings," as the subjectivist must indeed do if he is to avoid the different objection that I may make a true ethical judgement without actually feeling an emotion of approval or disapproval at the time I make the judgement or just before. It is indeed less difficult to suppose that, when a man makes a wrong ethical judgement (other than one which turns merely on a question of means), he is always mistaken about his unconscious tendencies to have feelings than that he is always mistaken about the present feelings he has; but it still seems perfectly obvious that "A was wrong in judging p right or good" does not entail "A was mistaken as to his own psychological tendencies to have feelings about p." Perhaps he could not in fact change his opinion and recognise himself to have been mistaken without a change in (not a mistake about) the tendencies in question, but this is quite a different point. The remaining objections are still less affected by this amendment.

It may still be true that the agent is often, though by no means always, the only person capable of judging with adequate assurance that it is right for him to do A rather than B. For he alone knows his own nature and state of mind, and these are often data highly relevant to the rightness or wrongness of an act. But this does not prove that his thinking the act right is the sole circumstance which makes it right, unless the fact that I am the only person who can remember what I felt like on a certain occasion a month ago proves that my feelings at that time were caused by my remembering them now.

Thwarted in their attempts to make "ethical judgements" merely autobiographical, subjectivists have commonly taken to maintaining that they are really commands, wishes, or exclamations. In that case they are neither true nor false and so are not judgements at all, though for the sake of convenience in terminology I shall use the phrase "ethical judgements" in inverted commas to cover such a view, meaning by "judgements" here real or apparent judgements. To say that "ethical judgements" are exclamations is to say that they are expressions of emotion, but this is distinguished from saying that they are judgements about the speaker's emotions. To say

"Alas!" is not, it may be contended, to assert, though it is to suggest, that I am in distress. This solution has been rightly challenged on the ground that it must be admitted at any rate that ethical expressions are sentences deliberately constructed by the speaker to express his feelings, and voluntarily and deliberately to employ a form of language intended to express the fact that I have a particular kind of feeling can hardly be distinguished from asserting that I have the feeling in question.[6]

The criticism could be met only if it were held that all ethical expressions were merely involuntary exclamations like "Ou!" But it is certain that many ethical expressions, so far from being mere involuntary cries, are made only after careful deliberation and with the conscious purpose of conveying something believed to be true. These cases at any rate are not covered by the theory in question, even if there are some other cases which it does cover. I should indeed maintain that the theory was not true of any ethical expressions, for I do not see how mere involuntary exclamations could be regarded as *ethical* expressions even if they included words like "good" or "right." As Professor Broad has just pointed out,[7] there is more than a verbal difference between saying "I have an emotion" and merely exclaiming because I have it, but there is not between saying that I have an emotion and deliberately exclaiming with the purpose of telling people that I have it. No doubt, when I exclaim with this purpose, I may have in mind something other than the mere communication of a truth about my emotions, but so I may if I state, for example, that I am sorry about so-and-so.

If this argument is justified the exclamational view of such judgements is indistinguishable from the autobiographical view; that is, the view that ethical judgements are judgements

---

[6] E. F. Carritt, *Philosophy*, Vol. XIII, No. 50, p. 133.
[7] *Philosophy*, Vol. XXI, No. 79, p. 101.

about the speaker's feelings, and falls before the objections which we have just brought against that type of view, so that it is perhaps not really worth while discussing it by itself. But, even if this argument were invalid and the two views could be distinguished, we could urge against the exclamational view most of the objections brought against the other. We could still object that, if I say something is bad and you say it is good, we are sometimes contradicting each other. We could point out that it is incompatible with the place which argument and citation of empirical facts have in ethics. We could urge that for me to make a moral judgement about, for example, Hitler is not merely to express my own psychological state. We could insist that, when I ask for advice on an ethical point, all that I am wanting or should want is not just to have my emotions affected. That the view would make it impossible for an "ethical judgement" to be true or false at all is a more fundamental objection which does not apply to the autobiographical view. If "ethical judgements" are neither true nor false, not only would such "judgements" not be strictly provable (which may be admitted in any case), but nothing whatever could be said in their support. For to say something in their support would be to say something which makes their truth more likely, but they can no more be true according to this view than a blow can be true. Now that in making "ethical judgements" we are at least claiming to assert what is true is surely obvious from a consideration of our psychological attitude when we make them. When I try to decide what I ought to do in a given case I am conscious of trying *to find out something*, not merely of feeling in a certain way, or resolving, or wanting to do something, or trying to produce a certain state of mind in myself, and "to try to find something out" is to try to discover what is true. There is commonly an emotive aspect to ethical judgements, that is, they express feelings as well as make an objective truth claim; but they cannot be confined to the former function. The only case of which I can think where this aspect is almost the sole one is when a man uses terms of abuse in sheer anger without the least consideration whether they are justified or not but calls somebody names without really meaning what he says. In such an instance he might equally well have said "Damn him!" as "He is a cad," but it is obvious that there is a great difference between these cases and a genuine ethical judgement. Again, we can hardly avoid admitting that "All acts done out of a desire to give pain as such are wrong" entails the judgement "If this act is done out of such a desire, it is wrong," and how could this be so if they were not propositions, and therefore true or false, instead of being mere commands, wishes, or explanations? Nor do I see how either form of the subjectivist theory could be reconciled satisfactorily with the important part played by reasoning and consistency in ethics when we are, for example, deciding what is just and what is not. Though it goes too far, the coherence theory of ethics has, as we shall see, shown that ethics has more affinity to logic than subjectivists could allow.

The same type of objections seems to me valid against the view that "moral judgements" really express wishes. The view that they are commands or exhortations is in some respects in a different position. For, firstly, a command or exhortation deliberately expressed in language can be distinguished from a statement that I have or tend to have certain feelings. Secondly, the view is not open to the objection that no two people would then ever mean the same thing by an "ethical judgement," since two persons can issue the same command in a sense in which they could not be said to have the same feelings or the same wish. But the view would still imply that no "ethical judgements" claim to be either true or false. Some people do not find this as incredible as I do; but I can only say that, when I look seriously at what I am doing when I make what is ordinarily called an ethical judgement, it is as plain to me that I am asserting what I think to be true, and not merely wishing, commanding, or exclaiming, as it is when I assert that "two plus two is four" or "there is a table in this room." Since we are talking at present about what sentences with ethical terms in them commonly mean I do not see how I can possibly go behind this introspective evidence. To mean is to intend to assert, and if I do not know when I intend to assert something and when I do not nobody else can. It is theoretically possible that I may be peculiar in my moral experience; but I do not think that I shall be taking any undue risks if I assume that the mode of experience known as "moral judgement" is not fundamentally and generically different in me from what it is in other people, though their theories about it may be in some cases very different from my own. In speaking of the view that "moral judgements" are commands or exhortations I mean here commands or exhortations of the person making the "judgement"; if it is held that they are commands of society or of God, we have different (though still objectionable) views which leave them the status of propositions that claim objectivity and that can be true. To command is not to assert a proposition, but that somebody has in fact issued a command is a proposition which can be true or false, so the two last views mentioned, though they are liable to other objections, are not open to the charge of subjectivism.

There are plenty of other objections to the command theory besides the objection that it would make "ethical judgements" neither true nor false. There is nothing specifically moral about a command. I may command something which I know or believe to be wrong, and I may quite well think you ought to do something which I should not dream of commanding you to do, for example, punish me. Nor is there anything moral about obeying a person just because he issues a command. If we obey him for a moral reason, for example, because we have given a promise, it is a reason over and above the command. So "You ought to do" cannot mean "I command or exhort you to do," because this would put you under no obligation. Even while I was giving the command, I should be aware that I must back it up by some additional reason which rendered obedience in this instance a duty or at least a matter of prudence. The knowledge that you ought to do something is sufficient in so far as you are moral to make you do it, the knowledge that I command you is not. If it were said in reply that a "moral judgement" is not a command to others but to oneself, then every resolution of mine to do anything would be a judgement that I ought to do it, which is clearly not the case, since I may resolve with great fervour to do something which I believe to be wrong. We could only develop the command theory in this way if we made a distinction between moral and non-moral or immoral resolves and begged the question by calling only the former commands. The command view is also open to the objection, brought against other subjective views, that it would entail the conclusion that, when one person asserts an action to be right and another asserts it to be wrong, what they say is not logically incompatible.

If it is maintained, as by Professor Stevenson in his recent book, *Ethics and Language*, that "ethical judgements" are partly judgements about the speaker's psychology claiming to be true and partly the expressions of emotive attitudes, including under this some kind of command or exhortation, the force of my objections is not diminished. The objections to the autobiographical view are objections which, if they show anything, show that the element in "ethical judgements" which is capable of being true or false is not merely autobiographical, and therefore they will not be removed by the theory that there is another element in "ethical judgements" which is not true or false at all. The element capable of being true or false, let us call it the "propositional element," cannot be merely autobiographical, because it may be false without the person judging having made a mistake about his own psychology, because it may be either the same as or logically incompatible with the propositional element in another person's judgement, when he condemns or approves the same thing, because arguments which are not relevant to conclusions about my psychology are relevant to the truth of this propositional element, because I might be uncertain whether the propositional element in my ethical judgement was true and yet certain that the autobiographical proposition to which it was claimed to reduce it was true, because it is clear that when I, for instance, judge that Hitler was a bad man or acted wrongly, I am asserting a proposition about Hitler and not merely about myself, though I am no doubt also expressing myself. So my objections are totally unaffected by the question whether or not there is another element in "ethical judgements" besides the propositional.[8]

At least two recent writers, Professor Kraft [9] and Professor Stace,[10] have attempted, while retaining the command theory, to secure a kind of universality for ethics by attributing to the commands expressed in "ethical judgements" a dependence on universal human desires such that to obey the command is a means to the attainment of what none of us can help desiring. Stace, at least at the time he wrote the book in question, held that the sentence "You ought to do this" is indistinguishable from the command "Do this," but added that the validity of the command for a person depends on the action commanded being an essential means or the most effective means to the

---

[8] For reply that it means "I should have done so but for irrelevant motives" v. below, p. 61.

[9] *Die Grundlagen einer wissenschaftlichen Wertlehre*, Springer, Vienna, 1937.

[10] *The Concept of Morals*, Macmillan, New York, 1937.

fulfilment of his desires. He then derives moral laws binding on all human beings from a consideration of the fact that human beings all desire happiness, which he thinks experience shows can best be attained by acting unselfishly. (He sharply distinguishes happiness from pleasure.) Similarly, Kraft says [11] that the imperatives which are commonly called value judgements, though not, strictly speaking, true or false, and therefore not judgements in the ordinary sense, yet may be universal and necessary in the ethical sense if (a) the action commanded is a causally necessary means for the satisfaction of a need or desire, (b) this need or desire is universal in human beings, (c) men are determined to have the need satisfied or the desire fulfilled. He is, I think, more logical than Stace in recognising that universality is in that case a matter of degree, because we can never be sure that there are no men who constitute exceptions to any psychological generalisation about human beings.

Such views come very near to analysing "ought to be done" as "is the best means to satisfy desire." A distinction is indeed made between truth and validity, and it is contended that a command cannot be true or false, but only "valid." But I do not see what the statement that a command is valid can mean except that it is legally or morally obligatory to carry it out, which does not take us much further. If commands cannot be true and to say "A ought to do so-and-so" is just a command, it cannot ever be true that anybody ought to do anything. However, since it is admitted that we are under no obligation to obey commands unless they are valid and they are held not to be valid unless obedience to them is a necessary means to the fulfilment of desires, this practically amounts to analysing judgements which assert an "ought" as simply judgements about the right means to the production of what is desired. Such a view would be naturalist, but not subjectivist, unless

---

[11] Op. cit., pp. 192–3.

it were held, as by Stace, that the desires on which the validity
of the commands depends are only one's own desires, and
not the desires of men in general. This seems to me a particularly unplausible form of subjectivism, since moral obligation presents itself so obviously as independent of the agent's
own desires except in so far as the latter happen to be an
indirect indication that the action is likely to produce good
results, and since it would commit us to a theory of complete ethical egoism. The desire theory is discussed in the next
chapter in its general non-subjectivist form.[12]

So far I have been discussing what sentences appearing to
make ethical statements mean. But I should not have gained
much by refuting the subjectivist views as to this if it could
be shown that there are conclusive arguments, if not for a
subjectivist analysis, at any rate against the view that ethical
propositions could be reasonably held to be true of anything.
I should then indeed be worse off than the person who accepted a subjectivist analysis, since I should have to hold that
all our ethical judgements were false or at least quite unjustified, while he may say that they still quite properly fulfil the
function for which they are really intended, that is, to express
the speaker's state of mind, or even, on one form of the theory,
that they are true—that is, of the speaker's psychology. So let
us now examine the case against the objectivity of ethical
judgements. If it is conclusive we shall have to be subjectivists
in the sense that we shall have to admit the impossibility of
making any true or at least any justified ethical judgements,
even if we do not admit that ethical judgements are of such
a nature that they could not conceivably be true at all or true
of anything but the mental state or dispositions of the speaker.

One argument is based on the striking differences in ethical
views between different people. But the differences between
the views of savages and those of modern scientists about

---

[12] V. below, pp. 62 ff.

eclipses, or between the views of different politicians as to the causes and likely effects of contemporary events, are as great as the differences between the views of savages and of Christians, or the views of democrats and of Nazis, as to ethics. Are we to conclude from this that the scientists are no more right than the savages or that the political events about which the disputes turn have not objectively any causes or effects? If we do not draw this conclusion here, why draw the corresponding conclusion about ethics? There are also various ways of explaining the differences of view that exist without casting doubt on the objectivity of ethics. In the first place, acts which bear the same name may be very different acts in different states of society, because the circumstances and the psychology of the people concerned are very different. So it might be the case that, for example, slavery or polygamy was right, as the course which involved least evil, in certain more primitive societies and wrong in ours. This is quite compatible with the objectivity of ethical judgements. The proposition that slavery was right in ancient Egypt would not contradict the proposition that it was wrong in the United States in 1850 A.D. Both we and the ancient Egyptians may be right in our ethical judgements. Let us, however, take cases where one party is wrong. Now it is important to note that differences in ethical beliefs are often due to differences of opinion as to matters of fact. If A and B differ as to the likely consequences of an action, they may well differ as to whether the action is right or wrong, and this is perhaps the most fertile source of disputes as to what is right. But it is not an ethical difference at all; it is a difference such as arises between rival scientific predictions based on inductive evidence. Differences or apparent differences of opinion of these two kinds obviously constitute no possible argument against the objectivity of ethics.

But there are also genuine ethical differences—that is, differences as to our judgements not of fact but of value. These may sometimes be explained by differences in people's experience of life. If I never experience A, I cannot realize the intrinsic goodness of A and may therefore wrongly subordinate it to something less good. And we must remember that what is intrinsically good is not a physical thing or a physical act, but the experience or state of mind associated with it. Even a long study of philosophical books would not qualify a person to pass a judgement on the intrinsic value of philosophy if he were hopelessly bad at the subject, because then, however many books he read, he would not have a genuinely philosophical experience. Two persons who differ as to the aesthetic value of a picture may really be judging about different things, their several experiences of it. Or at least their judgements will be based on different data. Other differences of view may be due to the misapplication of principles previously accepted, or to genuine intellectual confusions such as the philosopher or even the man of common sense who is not a philosopher could remove. For instance a man may confuse badness and wrongness and conclude or assume, for example, that, because he really sees lying to be always bad (an evil), he sees it to be always wrong, while it may be a case of choosing the lesser evil rather than the greater. Often a man will think that he knows intuitively P to be R when he really only sees it to be Q but confuses Q with R.

Or the judgement that something is good or bad on the whole may have been due to concentrating attention on one side of it while ignoring or underestimating the other sides, as, for instance, militarists concentrate their attention on the unselfish heroism which war brings out in men and forget or underestimate war's evils. Lesser degrees of such onesidedness it is impossible to avoid, and yet they may detrimentally influence ethical judgements. To decide what is right in a particular case is often a difficult matter of balancing the good or evil likely to be produced by one proposed act against that likely to be produced by others. For, even if we do not hold the view that the rightness of an act depends solely on its consequences, we cannot in any case deny that such balancing of the consequences should play the predominant part in at least many ethical decisions. Perhaps, if we foresaw all the consequences clearly as they would be in their factual character and could keep our attention fixed equally on them all, we should always be in agreement as to the degree in which they were good or evil as compared with the consequences of other possible acts. But, apart from the difficulty of estimating what the consequences of an act will be, it is practically impossible in cases which are at all complex to keep our attention sufficiently fixed at the same time on all the foreseeable consequences likely to be seriously relevant for good or evil, and so we are likely through lack of attention to underestimate the value or disvalue of some as compared to that of others.

The lack of attention I have mentioned is in some degree inevitable, but it is greatly enhanced by the influence of desire and prejudice. It is a commonplace that ethical mistakes are often due to non-intellectual factors. Whether these act only through affecting the attention or whether they can lead to mistaken valuations even in the presence of full attention to the object valued we need not discuss. Their influence is certainly not confined to ethical mistakes; we may note the different conclusions as to the factual consequences of a policy which members of different political parties may draw from the same evidence. There is in any case a large class of errors for which some form of "psychoanalysis" (I do not say necessarily the Freudian) is required rather than argument, and another (probably much larger) of which it can be said only that the person in question fell into error because he did not steadfastly will to seek the truth and therefore did not fix his attention on points which displeased him. The convictions of some people as to the objectivity of ethics appear to have been shaken by the fact that enthusiastic Nazis seem to have believed that it was their duty to do things which we are convinced are completely wrong, such as ill-treating the Jews; but is there any reason to think that these Nazis really wanted to arrive at the truth regarding the question whether it was right or wrong to send Jews to concentration camps? If not, we need not be so surprised that they did not attain the truth which they did not seek.

So it may well be the case that all differences in people's judgements whether certain actions are right or wrong or certain things good or bad are due to factors other than an irreducible difference in ethical intuition. But, even if they should not be, we must remember that ethical intuition, like our other capacities, is presumably a developing factor and therefore may be capable of error. But in any case we have said enough to show that great differences of opinion as to ethics are quite compatible with the objectivity of ethical judgements.

Differences between philosophers about the general theory of ethics are remarkably great; but experience shows that very wide philosophical differences are quite compatible with striking agreement as regards the kind of action judged right or wrong, just as radical differences between philosophers in their theory of perception and of physical objects are quite compatible with complete agreement in ordinary life as to what particular physical objects are in a particular place at a particular time. The differences between philosophers are differences not mainly as to their ethical judgements in concrete ethical situations, but as to the general theory explaining these. We may add that the differences between different peoples and different civilisations as to concrete ethical judgements are commonly exaggerated. David Livingstone says that nowhere had he need to teach the African savages at any rate the ethical, as opposed to the religious, portion of the Decalogue. But there is of course a great inconsistency (not only among savages) in confining to a limited group rules which demand universal extension.

Another argument is that ethical beliefs can be explained psychologically as having originated from non-ethical factors such as fear of punishment. Now there must be a psychological history of the origin of any beliefs, and there must have been a time when no ethical ideas or beliefs yet existed, both in the history of the individual and in the history of the race. But this does not prove that ethical beliefs originated solely from the pre-existing ideas through a sort of confusion and were not due to a genuine cognition of properties really present. There was also a time when there were no logical or mathematical ideas, but nobody would entertain a similar argument against logic or mathematics.

Further, to be sceptical about ethics on the strength of a theory as to the origin of ethical ideas would be to give up the more for the far less certain, indeed the extremely uncertain. For such a sceptical theory would rest on the psychology of children if applied to individual development, and the psychology of savages if applied to the evolutionary development of the race. But, owing to the impossibility of obtaining reliable introspective evidence, the psychology of children and savages, at least when we consider their higher mental processes or the beginnings of such, is speculative in the extreme. To quote from Broad, "Of all branches of empirical psychology that which is concerned with what goes on in the minds of babies must, from the nature of the case, be one of the most precarious. Babies, whilst they remain such, cannot tell us what their experiences are; and all statements made by grown persons about their own infantile experiences on the basis of ostensible memory are certainly inadequate and probably distorted. The whole of this part of psychology therefore is, and will always remain, a mere mass of speculations about infantile mental processes, put forward to explain certain features in the lives of grown persons and incapable in principle of any independent check or verification. Such speculations are of the weakest kind known to science." [13] The psychology of primitive savages is in an equally or almost equally weak position. Some of our ethical judgements, on the other hand, I should insist, are quite or almost as certain as any judgement, and, even if the reader is not prepared to go so far, he must admit that they are at any rate far more certain than could be any theory founded on the psychology of children and savages which explained them away. The same uncertainty must attach to any theory of ethics or analysis of ethical terms based on the way in which children learn the use of the terms. Such a theory is irrelevant unless it is based on a study of what children exactly have in mind and what their mental processes are when they use the words, and how can we possibly have a well founded idea of that when they cannot introspect or adequately report introspections?

Westermarck contends that objectivity is disproved by the fact that ethical judgements are based on emotion; [14] but he does not even try, as far as I can see, to disprove the view that emotions only provide a psychological condition in the absence of which we should not have been in a fit state ever to intuit the characteristic of goodness or the relation of obligation. I certainly should not admit that the emotion was normally or originally prior to at least a confused apprehension of good or evil, rightness or wrongness; but even if I, like some even among the objectivists and non-naturalists, admitted this and made the feeling of the emotion a necessary prior condition of the apprehension, Westermarck's conclu-

---

[13] *Mind*, Vol. LIII, No. 212, p. 354.
[14] *Ethical Relativity*, p. 60.

sion would not follow. The making of an ethical judgement will in any case presuppose various psychological conditions, but it does not follow that the judgement must be about these conditions. Nobody would argue that ethical judgements must all really be about breathing because breathing is a necessary condition without which we could not have made the judgements. Professor Brandt [18] argues that the laws governing changes in our ethical judgements are derivative from the laws of emotional phenomena in general, but he succeeds only in showing that emotional conditions lead to many errors and non-rational changes of opinion in ethics. It may be urged that ethical terms must at any rate have some connection with emotions and emotional dispositions, and this I am not prepared altogether to deny; but the connection I envisage and of which I shall speak later is certainly not one which supports any form of subjectivism.

Westermarck has another argument against the objectivity of ethical judgements, which seems to be due to a downright confusion. He argues that moral judgements cannot be true because there are degrees of goodness, badness, etc., but there are no degrees of truth.[19] But, if this argument were valid, it would surely prove equally that there could be no true judgements about the size or temperature of an object. He seems to have confused the assertion that it is true that something has a property in a greater or lesser degree with the assertion that truth itself has degrees. He is not even consistent, for, being himself a naturalist rather than a subjectivist, he does ascribe truth to ethical judgements as assertions about the usual feelings of people, although feelings vary in degree.

But probably the principal reason which makes people inclined to deny the objectivity of ethics is the fact that in ethical argument we are very soon brought to a point where

---

[18] *Ethics*, Vol. LII, p. 65.
[19] *Ethical Relativity*, p. 218.

we have to fall back on intuition, so that disputants are placed in a situation where there are just two conflicting intuitions between which there seem to be no means of deciding. However, it is not only ethics but all reasoning which presupposes intuition. I cannot argue A, ∴ B, ∴ C without seeing that A entails B and B entails C, and this must either be seen immediately or require a further argument. If it is seen immediately, it is a case of intuition; [17] if it has to be established by a further argument, this means that another term, D, must be interpolated between A and B such that A entails D and D entails B, and similarly with B and C, but then the same question arises about A entailing D, so that sooner or later we must come to something which we see intuitively to be true, as the process of interpolation cannot go on *ad infinitum*. We cannot therefore, whatever we do, get rid of intuition if we are to have any valid inference at all. It may, however, be said that in subjects other than ethics people at any rate agree in their intuitions. But outside mathematics or formal logic this is by no means universally true. There is frequent disagreement about matters of fact as to what has happened or will happen or concerning the causes of something, and when we have exhausted the arguments on a given point in these matters there still remains a difference between the ways in which these arguments are regarded by the disputants. In any science where you cannot prove your conclusions but only make them more or less probable there will be different estimates as to the balance of probability. As in ethics you have to balance different values against each other in order to decide what you ought to do, so here you have to balance different probable arguments, and in order to do this you must rely at some point or other on an estimate of their

---

[17] This proposition is not convertible: I include under "intuition" cases where some mediation is required but insight goes beyond anything that could be strictly proved by the mediation.

strength which cannot itself be further justified by mediate reasoning. Yet, when everything has been said in the way of argument, people may not all agree. Some will attribute more weight to one consideration, others to another, as they do in ethical questions about what is the right action in a given case. Our decision as to which of two probable arguments is the stronger may be influenced by other arguments in turn; but in order to deal with the situation rationally we must also estimate the weight of these other arguments, so that in the last resort it is a matter of insight into their nature which cannot be settled by other arguments *ad infinitum*. Just as in a demonstrative argument you must see intuitively how each step follows from the preceding one, so in the case of a probable argument you must rely on estimates of the degree of probability given by the argument as compared to that given by arguments on the other side, and these estimates, unless the degree of probability can be mathematically calculated, must either be themselves intuitive or be deduced from other estimates which are intuitive. I do not wish to maintain that reasoning in these matters is altogether analogous to that which occurs in dealing with ethical questions, but at any rate it is the case here that, as in ethics, we are often confronted with a situation in which we either see or do not see, and cannot logically prove, that what we seem to see is true. Yet we cannot surely therefore conclude that the scientific or historical propositions under discussion are really only propositions about the state of mind of the people who assert them, or that they are neither true nor false, or that we have no justification whatever for believing any of them!

We must therefore have intuition, and in a subject where infallibility is not attainable intuitions will sometimes disagree. Some philosophers indeed prefer not to call them intuitions when they are wrong, but then the problem will be to distinguish real from ostensible intuitions, since people certainly sometimes think they see intuitively what is not true. Now Earl Russell says: "Since no way can be even imagined for deciding a difference as to values, the conclusion is forced upon us that the difference is one of tastes, not one as to any objective truth"; [18] but what I have said shows that we can imagine plenty of ways. I have indicated that errors as to judgements of value may arise (a) from lack of the requisite experience, (b) from intellectual confusions of some sort, (c) from failure to attend adequately to certain aspects of the situation or of the consequences, or (d) from psychological causes such as those with which the psychoanalyst deals. Therefore to remove errors we may (a) supply the lacking experience, or failing this, if possible, describe it in a way which will make its nature clear to the other party; we may (b) dispel intellectual confusions by making adequate distinctions or exposing actual fallacies such as make a person think he has seen that A is C when he has really only seen that A is B and mistakenly identified B with C; we may (c) suggest the direction of attention to the neglected points, or we may (d) use psychological methods. And we shall, if we are wise, also look out to see whether we ourselves have tripped up in any of these ways. Further, even when inference cannot completely prove or disprove, we may use it to confirm or cast doubt on ostensible intuition. The large class of errors which result mainly from an unwillingness really to seek for the truth can hardly be used as an argument against objectivity, since they are due to the moral fault of the persons who are in error and could have been removed if the latter had tried. In these cases the trouble is not that there are no means of deciding but that the means are not used.

The methods I have suggested will not always be successful, but then is there any sphere in which human efforts always do succeed? Even the methodology of physical science cannot

---

[18] *Religion and Science*, p. 250.

lay down rules which will guarantee that any scientist can make discoveries or show him in detail in advance how to prove to others the truth of the discoveries when made. I am not claiming that it is possible in practice to remove all ethical differences, but how do we know that it could not be done if there were a will on each side to listen to what the other had to say and an intelligence to discern the best methods to adopt in order to facilitate a decision? A person cannot be brought into agreement even with the established truths of science if he will not listen to what the scientist says, and there is no reason to think even with ethical intuition that there are not describable processes by which any cause of error can on principle be removed. I insert the words "on principle" simply because it will still often be the case that none of the disputants thinks of the right way of removing the error or that the person in error will not or cannot take it, as also occurs in disputes about questions of fact outside ethics.

Where the intuitive belief is due to non-intellectual factors of a kind which vitiate it, there seem to be two possibilities of cure. First, the person concerned may lose all tendency to hold the intuitive conviction when its alleged cause is clearly pointed out to him. The alleged cause is then in his case probably at least an essential part of the real cause. If, on the other hand, the intuitive belief remains unimpaired, and the man does not react to the causal explanation in a way which suggests that it has really touched a sore point, this is presumptive evidence that the explanation is mistaken. But, secondly, the cure from a false belief due to non-intellectual factors is more likely to arise because the man has been induced to approach the subject in a new spirit than merely because the true causation of the belief has been suggested to him. After all it is impossible to prove even to an unprejudiced person that such a causal theory as to the origin of a person's belief is really correct. How to induce a person to make such a new approach is a question not of logical argument but of practical psychology.

We must not think of intuition as something quite by itself, uninfluenced by inference; it is helped by inference but sees beyond what could be proved by inference. And, when intuitive ethical views differ, use may be made of inference to support one or other of the clashing views, especially by showing that it fits well into a coherent ethical system. This will not settle the question absolutely conclusively, but it can help toward settlement. Perhaps as the result of the inference one of the parties to the dispute may realize that he does not see by intuition what he claimed to see, but something rather different. It would thus be a great mistake to say that, when two men disagree on an ethical question, there is nothing to be done about it or that there is no scope in ethics for inference. No argument is available which could prove the subjectivity or fallaciousness of all ethics without establishing a similar conclusion about all other branches of study except mathematics and formal logic.

This leaves the sceptical view still unrefuted; but we have removed the main motives for its acceptance, and there remains just the gratuitous possibility that our ethical judgements may all be mistaken. We may reply by asking whether it is even a possibility. Do we not *know* that some (not of course all) of our ethical judgements are true? Do I not *know* that it would be wrong of me to go into the street and torture the first person I met even if I happened to be so constituted that I should enjoy watching his sufferings? And if we must admit absolutely certain knowledge of even one ethical proposition, have we not disposed of the sceptic? If we must admit at least almost certain knowledge, is it not almost certain that we have disposed of the sceptic? I think this answer is quite right, but the sceptic will not take it. He will say: "However certain you are in your ethical judgements you may be wrong, and I cannot therefore accept them till you have proved them to be true." Now I just cannot believe that our ethical judgements are all mistaken, and I suspect that nobody really does believe it when they are concerned with practical issues. But I cannot prove by any formal logic that I am right in my view. An opponent may admit that the naturalist and subjectivist accounts do not give any adequate analysis of ethical judgements and yet maintain that these judgements, in so far as they assert anything more than is given in such an analysis, are false, or that at least there is no justification for believing them to be true. On the other hand, he cannot possibly prove that I am wrong, and now that the positive arguments for subjectivism have been removed I think that the *onus probandi* is on him.

This brings us to a fundamental cleavage in philosophy, a great parting of the ways. There are a number of different kinds of field where we have from the commonsense point of view what anybody would ordinarily call knowledge and yet are quite unable to give arguments which *prove* it really to be so. This occurs in the case of memory, in the case of minds other than one's own, in the case of induction, and in the case of ethics. In all these cases the philosophers have despite repeated efforts not succeeded in giving a proof which provides anything like general satisfaction, so if we are determined to be sceptical we can without logical absurdity decline to believe any and every proposition that falls within the field in question. This course is consistent, but it is very difficult to find a philosopher who has taken it throughout and it would be still more difficult to find one who really thought like this in daily life. Some phi'osophers have indeed tried to make the best of both worlds by maintaining that the propositions in question were true but analysing them in such a way as to satisfy the sceptic. For instance, it has been said that propositions about other minds are true but are merely about one's own sense data, and it has been said that ethical propositions are true but are only statements about one's own feelings. A view like this seems to me to be still more incredible, since it not only maintains the sceptical position in effect, though not in words, but makes out that the plain man is himself a sceptic. No doubt it is a little less incredible to most people in some of these fields than in others, for example, subjectivist ethics is not so incredible as solipsism, but either seems to me to be the sort of thing one could not seriously believe for an hour in the emergencies of daily life. And I demand of a philosophy that it should be in accord with what we cannot possibly help believing in ordinary life. No doubt it may criticise our commonsense beliefs in detail and improve the concepts involved by clarification, but if it throws them overboard altogether it is destroying its own basis and condemning itself to vacuity. For a philosopher cannot in his epistemology have any basis but the cases of knowledge and reasonable belief in ordinary life. He can deny the truth of these only on the strength of philosophical arguments which will hardly be as certain as the propositions which they are used to deny. Even Earl Russell admitted that "all knowledge must be built up upon our instinctive beliefs, and if these are rejected, nothing is left." [19] But certainly our instinctive beliefs include ethical ones.

The position of the absolute ethical sceptic is analogous to that of the absolute theoretical sceptic. The theoretical sceptic cannot be refuted, unless we admit that it is a refutation to point to propositions which we cannot possibly help believing but cannot prove by argument; and of course he may talk if he likes, but he cannot without inconsistency claim that any of his statements are rationally justified. Similarly, the complete sceptic as to values cannot be refuted, except by pointing

---

[19] *Problems of Philosophy*, p. 39. I should not, however, commit myself to his terminology.

to value propositions which we cannot help believing but cannot prove by argument, a kind of refutation which, though I think it valid, he would never admit. Further, just as the theoretical sceptic can still talk, so the ethical sceptic can still act in accordance with his desires, but he cannot consistently claim that there is any justification for any of his acts, that any one is more rational than any other. If it is retorted that, even if we grant an objective "ought," we might be equally said to require a reason why we should do what we ought, the reply is that the ought is itself a reason so that there is no further room for question left, just as there is no sense in asking why we should believe what is shown to be true. People who ask why they should do what they ought either are confused, or they are really asking what it is about the particular act in question which makes it the act they ought to do, or they are wanting to know what good they will obtain for themselves by doing it. The last question brings in a different kind of reason from the moral reason, namely a prudential reason, but (though not such a satisfactory reason as an answer to the problem of obligation) it is still a reason founded on the notion of good.

Some people forget that not only specifically moral acts but even mere acts of ordinary prudence in furtherance of one's own interests presuppose the abandonment of the sceptic's position. The sceptic as to values is not entitled to believe even the proposition that it is more reasonable to wash his hands in water than in sulphuric acid, for this presupposes at any rate that pain is evil. So he has no real ground for not washing his hands in sulphuric acid. To say that he does not like to do so is to give a psychological cause and not a reason, unless we assume that it is *good* to do what one likes or that our desires ought to be satisfied. It is not possible to prove even that our own pain is evil; and if we admit even this judgement to be self-evidently true, there are other judgements as to values, such as that we are under some obligation to further the good of others, which are as evidently true, so that it is inconsistent to accept the first and reject the second. If we trust our intuitive awareness of values in the one case we are equally justified in trusting it in the others; if we were to reject it in the one case we should have no less call to reject it in the others. And if the sceptic demands for judgements in ethics a logical proof as we have in mathematics, or an empirical inductive proof as we have in natural science, he is condemning ethics because ethical cognition is not like other kinds of cognition but has its own distinctive nature, which is like condemning empirical evidence because it is not mathematical or mathematical proof because it is not empirical. As Aristotle says, it is a mark of lack of intelligence to demand in a given subject arguments of a kind which that subject does not admit. It is not a question of meeting the sceptic by metaphysical or epistemological arguments which fall outside ethics or by considerations of general probability, but of returning to one's conviction in concrete ethical cases. If we attend to actual concrete ethical problems we cannot at the time of attention be sceptics, and what we see when actually considering ethical problems is the first consideration in framing a theory of ethics. Even professed subjectivists in ethics regard some acts as unreasonable in the sense of imprudent and express strong *moral* opinions against others.

Such is the reluctance of serious thinkers to adopt a position of ethical scepticism that those who held that we have no right to claim truth for any ethical propositions which are anything more than psychological propositions about human desires or feelings have generally maintained, not that all ethical propositions are false, but that they are in fact merely propositions about human psychology. Rather than argue "They go beyond this, therefore they are false," they argued "They are true, therefore they cannot go beyond this." So they have adopted what, since Moore's *Principia Ethica*, has been called a "naturalist" analysis of ethical propositions. With this we shall deal in the next chapter, except in so far as some naturalist views have already been handled under the heading of subjectivism.

CHAPTER II

Naturalism

Let us now turn to naturalist views of ethics which are not subjectivist. Without dwelling on the intricacies of the definition of "natural" or "non-natural" as the terms appear in Moore's *Principia Ethica*, I think we may understand a naturalist view of ethics as one which, while admitting that ethical propositions are sometimes true, analyses ethical concepts solely in terms of the concepts of a natural science. This must involve making ethics potentially a mere branch of the science, though this latter point is not always realized. The science in question is usually psychology, but we must not identify a naturalist definition with a psychological definition. If anybody were silly enough to define "good" in terms of the concepts of physics or geology, it would still be a naturalist definition. But the only at all plausible naturalist definitions have been in terms of psychology, though there have also been attempts made at biological definitions. All definitions of ethical concepts in non-ethical terms are not, however, naturalist. A theological definition would not be, since God is not a concept of a natural science. The same applies to any metaphysical definition.

Denial of the possibility of a naturalist definition does not commit one to saying that value properties in other than an instrumental sense belong to anything but experiences, states of minds, or persons; but to say they belong only to psychological entities is not to say they are themselves psychological properties which we can discover by empirical introspection

36

or analysable completely in terms of such properties. Nor need a non-naturalist hold that there are no senses of words such as "good" and "ought" in respect of which a naturalist definition is allowable. All he need hold is that there are some senses which cannot be defined in such a way, especially the sense of "good" in which the word stands for "intrinsically good."

A naturalist view, as I said earlier, need not be subjectivist. If ethical propositions are regarded as propositions asserting only that most people, or people of a particular class, have certain feelings, or that certain things will satisfy them, they are still objective in the sense in which psychological generalisations of a non-ethical kind about human beings are objective. They do not depend for their validity on the subjective state of the person who asserts them. Non-subjective naturalist views are therefore exposed to a somewhat different type of criticism from that to which subjectivist theories are open. The alternative to a naturalist view is the view that, besides any elements which could be analysed in psychological terms or other terms appertaining to a natural science, ethical propositions include at least one concept which cannot be thus analysed. Since we are here talking of the analysis of propositions and not of the question whether they are true, it does not straightway follow that this "non-natural" concept applies to anything. It is logically possible to maintain that the concepts expressed by "good" and "ought" in the ethical sense are "non-natural" and yet that nothing is really good or really obligatory in this sense but only in a naturalist sense. In that case all our statements which use the terms "good" or "ought" in their ethical sense will be false in the most essential respect. Or, if the sceptic does not go so far, he may say that, though it is possible for anything we can tell that these non-natural properties really belong to something, we are not justified in asserting that they do. Thus a non-naturalist analysis may be combined with a subjectivist view in the sense in which the latter term stands for the position of the moral sceptic. This is a position that cannot be refuted either by a formal logical proof or by an appeal to introspection, since introspection by itself can only reveal what we have in mind and not what is true. But anyone who like myself finds it impossible to deny that there are some ethical propositions which we have a right to hold true will, if he rejects any naturalist analysis of ethical propositions, have to admit that there are experiences and actions which really have properties (goodness and obligatoriness) that cannot be reduced to psychological terms.

This is the importance of the question of the analysis of commonsense propositions. It does seem as if we know the truth of certain commonsense propositions; and, if so, when we have given their analysis we shall have also determined what is true of the objectively real. I have already towards the end of the last chapter said something about the position of the ethical sceptic. Though this sceptical position cannot be refuted logically, most people find it hard to accept it, and some have thought that they could avoid it and yet escape the admission of non-natural ethical concepts by giving a naturalist analysis of ethical propositions. If they can be convinced that such an analysis is impossible, they may, rather than become moral sceptics, admit the real existence of non-natural properties. So the interest of the question does not lie merely in determining what people think when they use ethical terms, but has a bearing on what is objectively true.

It is worth noting that, if someone both held that ethical propositions could not be analysed without introducing a non-natural concept and yet held that this non-natural concept, though present in our minds, did not apply to anything, he would have to admit that the human mind can create an idea of something which is neither itself given in any sort of experience nor composed of elements given in experience. Now, if my type of view is correct, though we must admit that ethical concepts are non-empirical in the sense of not being derived from sensation, we may still hold that we are immediately aware of the properties of goodness and obligatoriness as belonging to certain states of minds and actions, so that they are given in experience in a wider sense of that word. But they cannot be given in experience at all if they are not really properties or relations of anything, even of ourselves or of our own mental states. The notion of goodness in the intrinsic sense is in that case the notion of a property which does not belong to anything and the notion of obligation the notion of a relation which does not relate anything, yet we have ideas of intrinsic goodness and of obligation. If it turns out that they cannot be analysed in empirical, or any non-ethical terms, they are not compound ideas formed by putting together other ideas given in experience, nor can they, on the sceptical view, be the fruit of an intuitive insight into the real. But to have to admit that the human mind can thus form a new idea "off its own bat" is repugnant to most philosophers, and in a special degree to the type of empiricist philosopher who is inclined to deny the objectivity of ethics. It is an axiom for such thinkers that "the mind cannot create a new simple idea." The case is all the stronger because what is in question is not a determinate quality or relation under some determinable of which instances have already been experienced, but a new determinable of a quite unique kind. And in any case, if we have an idea of a relation or quality and it is irreducible, surely the most plausible explanation is that the relation or quality is given in some experience and is therefore really present in something if only in an experience (though this does not hinder us, when we have really found it present on some occasions, from thinking wrongly for some reason, for example, a false analogy, that it is present in others when it is really absent). How is the sceptic to explain our alleged mistake about obligation? He cannot well hold that it is a concept which has a right application some-where but is misapplied in being applied to ethics. The sug-gestion has been made to me [1] that relative obligation plainly occurs in experience, since we find by experience that, if we want to attain certain ends, we are obliged to behave in a certain way, and that we may have formed from this by a confusion the idea of absolute obligation which we apply in ethics, just as we confusedly thought, till we knew better, that there was an absolute and not only a relative "down." This explanation is, however, inadequate because the idea of moral obligation is radically different from that of "relative obligation" thus understood. For the latter only contains the notion of means to an end and is quite compatible with the end being known to be ethically evil. For instance, we can say that in this sense of "ought" Hitler "ought" to have invaded Britain after Dunkirk or that a murderer "ought" to have killed not only A but B to escape exposure, however evil we think such a deed would have been. From this the idea of ethical obliga-tion does not differ merely in respect of the absence of a relation but in respect of the presence of a totally new feature, the distinctive characteristic of the moral "ought." Anybody who disagrees with me in this must be referred to the argu-ments of the present chapter by which I try to disprove the view that "ought" is to be analysed in terms of conduciveness to objects of desire.

Two, as I think, fatal objections to any naturalist analysis are stated by Broad and Moore respectively. Broad points out that the logical consequence of a view which defines ethical concepts in psychological terms is "not (as with subjectivism) that in disputes on moral questions there comes a point beyond which we can only say '*De gustibus non est disputandum.*' " On the contrary "the logical consequence is that all such dis-putes *could* be settled, and that the way to settle them is to

---

[1] By R. Robinson.

collect statistics of how people do feel. And to me this kind of answer seems utterly irrelevant to this kind of question." [2] This objection, brought by Broad against the particular view of Hume, would apply to all forms of psychological natural- ism. For all such views would equate ethical propositions with propositions about the psychology of men in general or of some class of men and therefore with propositions the truth of which is capable of being determined in this way. We might put the argument even more strongly and say that such a view would make ethical propositions identical with vaguely expressed propositions about statistics. For the difference be- tween vagueness and definiteness is the only difference between saying "most" and saying "882 out of 1024." Yet ethical propositions, whatever they are, are surely not just vague propositions about statistics. Any biological definition would, I have no doubt, be open to the same objection. If, for example, we defined ethical conduct as what makes for survival we should have to mean by commending a practice ethically that the rate of increase of population was greater among those who adopted such a line of conduct than among those who did not.

Secondly, Moore objected to all naturalist definitions of "good" that, no matter what the alleged definition is, we can always see that it is quite sensible to ask whether something which has the property put forward in the definition is or is not good, and that therefore the definition is wrong. For, if it were right, to say that something which had the defining property was good would be to utter a tautology, and to question whether it was good would be to ask whether what is good is good.[3] This, I think, expresses a valid objection,

---

[2] C. D. Broad, *Five Types of Ethical Theory*, p. 115.
[3] *Principia Ethica*, § 13. When I quote from Moore I am not trying to give his present view, nor should I defend his detailed statement any more than he now would.

but one that must be used with care. Obviously, till we have made up our minds whether a particular definition of "good" is correct or not, it may still be a question the answer to which can seriously be doubted whether something which has the defining property is correctly called "good," and naturalists have thought that they could meet Moore's objection by raising this point. But surely the trouble with the naturalist definitions is that, when we consider them and ask if what has the defining property is always good, we are clearly conscious that we are asking, not a question about what a term means, but the question whether everything which has the defining property has also a different property, signified by "good." It is not merely that it is an undecided question of definition, but that it is not a question of definition at all. The naturalist says that "good" means "desired" or "such that men feel approval" or "such as ultimately to satisfy men"; but it presents itself to us as, at least partly, a contingent question of empirical fact whether what is approved or desired or will ultimately satisfy us is also good. Perhaps men are so constituted that in fact they only desire or only feel approval of what is in some way good (provided they know what it is like), and perhaps they are so constituted that the good and only the good will ultimately satisfy them. But at least whether they are so constituted is a doubtful question the answer to which we could not know without enormously extensive and indeed unobtainable empirical information, and not one an affirmative answer to which follows from the very meaning of "good." We never, with any of the definitions which have been proposed, reach the stage at which it seems at all plausible (at least except for extraneous and, I think, wrong reasons) to hold that to say a thing is good is at all the same as to say that it has the defining property in question. But before we are entitled to accept a definition (in Moore's sense of the word) that stage must be reached.

As far as I can see, it is never possible to prove strictly that an analysis of a given concept is correct, though it may be possible to prove that one is incorrect. For, however clear it may be that AB always accompanies C and vice versa, somebody who nevertheless maintains that he can apprehend the property C as something distinct from AB can never be logically refuted, however unreasonable his attitude may be in a given instance. We can only ask ourselves carefully whether we do have this property C in mind as distinct from AB when we use the words. So in dealing with attempts at analysis we are in the last resort forced to fall back on our consciousness that a proposed analysis does or does not express what we mean. For, even if a philosophical analysis expresses something more than what we mean, it must at least include approximately all that we mean. It is true that an analysis may sometimes express what I mean when I think it does not, but I can never be justified in positively accepting an analysis as an expression of my meaning until I have reached the stage at which I can say: "Well, this is what I meant all along, although I did not put it so clearly." Now, in the case of naturalist definitions of "good," so far from my seeing this I see quite definitely the contrary. I see that propositions about what is good in some senses of "good" are propositions which cannot be analysed adequately in psychological terms; I see it almost as clearly as I see that they cannot be analysed adequately in terms of physics or mathematics. It is not merely that I have been unable to think of any naturalist definition which satisfied me but am prepared to leave it an open question whether somebody may not in the future think of one which would satisfy me. On the contrary I see that "good," "right," "duty," "ought," "morality" are just not the sort of concepts which can ever be analysed completely in terms of psychology, as I can see that sights cannot be analysed in terms of sounds (however many correlations we may establish between sights and sounds). This awareness is immediate, but it is a sort of immediate awareness which even a sceptically minded philosopher cannot rule out. For even such philosophers will admit the possibility of some introspection. "What I mean" is, in the case of propositions, "what I intend to assert," and I surely can sometimes be immediately aware of my own intentions. Merely to use the words on the right occasions is not to understand their meaning, unless we are prepared to adopt a purely behaviouristic account of human thought. There may be senses in which it is sometimes true to say that a man does not know what he means, but I could not use words intelligently if I were not, sometimes at least, immediately aware of my meaning. And if I am quite clear in my mind what I mean, I do not know how anybody else can get behind this and prove to me that I mean something else. For we are discussing at present not whether anything has a property of goodness that is not naturalistically definable but whether we are thinking of such a property when we assert ethical propositions.

Now, while it is theoretically possible that I may be peculiar in this respect and have a quite different kind of moral consciousness from other people, this supposition is in the highest degree unlikely, so that what I find when I investigate my own experiences is also evidence in regard to the experience of others. As a matter of fact the philosophers who give naturalist definitions of ethical terms do not, despite their predilection for empiricism, commend their conclusions as the direct result of a plain empirical investigation of our moral experience, but put these forward on the assumption that if they can find a hypothesis which will rid them of any concept different from those of the natural sciences they ought to accept it whether or not it seems introspectively plausible. This *a priori* assumption I can see no reason to make.

What arguments could be brought to show that I do not

mean what I think I mean? The most plausible perhaps is that, if goodness were, as Moore claimed, a simple property, it is strange that nobody had discovered this till the time of Sidgwick. If we are aware of such a simple property or concept, must we not know that we are aware of it? Now, as we shall see later on, I do not agree that goodness is simple and indefinable. All non-natural concepts need not be indefinable, provided they are definable in terms of some other non-natural concept. What I do maintain is that "goodness" cannot be defined wholly in non-ethical terms. The argument is indeed relevant to my position, since I am committed to holding that there is at least one indefinable ethical term. But, if "good" is really definable in any way, this would be an adequate reply to the argument about "good"; and while it is a matter of doubt whether many people have had an idea of the indefinable goodness, it is quite certain that people have for ages had a definite idea at least of an "ought" which was to them *prima facie* distinct from desire, fear, emotion, or any other psychological terms, thus giving at least one indefinable concept of ethics. We are not dealing with a property that only a few modern philosophers claim to discover but with one that is present in the thoughts of almost every man, so that the naturalist cannot possibly bring it forward as a positive argument for his view that people were not aware of the property in question till quite recently. And if there are difficulties in seeing how there could be all this dispute about a concept which is simple and can be recognised by immediate inspection, there are also difficulties in seeing how, if all ethical terms are definable non-ethically, there can be such wide divergencies of opinion as to what the definition is or whether there is a definition. Of the naturalists themselves two are rarely agreed on the same definition. A correct definition should give us what we mean by "good" or "ought," and how is it that there should be such widely different beliefs not only as to what is true but as to what we mean? If philosophers did not till recently commit themselves to the view that some ethical concept is simple and unanalysable, neither did they till recently, except in rare cases, commit themselves to a naturalist analysis of all ethical concepts. As a matter of fact the same sort of puzzle arises about any fundamental conception in regard to which there are philosophical disputes, and is not peculiar to ethics.

However, I think the disagreement in the case of ethics may be accounted for largely by the following circumstances:

(1) The naturalists, either because they have a general philosophical outlook which makes them unwilling to admit the existence of any characteristics which cannot be reduced to empirical terms, or for some other reason, think that we could never be justified in asserting that anything was good or bad, right or wrong, if we meant anything more by these statements than what could be analysed in psychological terms. They are therefore forced to hold either that our ethical judgements are analysable in such a fashion, or that these judgements are all mistaken or unjustified—and they prefer the first alternative. I doubt whether anybody would be inclined to analyse ethical judgements naturalistically if he considered merely his state of mind as it seemed to him in making such judgements, and was not influenced by other, epistemological considerations.

(2) Some writers have apparently confused the highly plausible view that value predicates in their basic senses are only applicable to psychological entities; that is, minds and their states, with the view that they are reducible to psychological properties empirically discoverable.

(3) There are some senses of "good" in which "good" might well be defined naturalistically. For example, "strawberries are good" may well equal "I like strawberries" or "I find the taste of strawberries pleasant." "This is a good knife" seems

to mean only that it is useful for certain purposes, which may be bad or indifferent; I should still call it a good knife even if it had not been used for anything except committing murders. Philosophers in the past have usually not paid sufficient attention to the multiplicity of senses in which the same word is used, so those who defined "good" naturalistically may easily have confused different senses of "good," though this is more likely to be the case with earlier than with contemporary naturalists, since more attention is now being paid to differences of meaning.

(4) Just as there are some senses of "good" which require a naturalist definition, so perhaps there are some senses of "definition" in which we might have a naturalist definition of every sense of "good." Colours could be said to be definable in terms of wave-lengths because they are correlated with them, but this would not commit one to saying that the colour as seen was just the wave-length which occurred in its definition or the property of being accompanied by such a wave-length. People knew what yellow was long before they knew anything about the wave-length. Similarly it might be possible in a sense to define "good" in terms of a characteristic which always accompanied goodness without holding that goodness just was the characteristic in question. I do not wish to commit myself to the view that such a universally accompanying characteristic could be found, but at least the view that there is such a characteristic is in some of its forms less unplausible than the view that this characteristic is identical with goodness. We must remember that the fact, if it be a fact, that A and BC go together is no proof that BC is identical with A. Suppose a future physiologist were, as is logically possible, to discover a specific modification of the brain which accompanied every good experience and action and never occurred without being accompanied by a good experience or action. The brain-modification would then be an infallible sign of

goodness, but it still certainly would not follow that "good" just *meant* "accompanied by this brain-modification" or that goodness *was identical with* the property of being accompanied by it. Till recently the different senses of "definition" have not been clearly distinguished, at least with reference to ethics, and even now the most prominent school of naturalist philosophers, the verificationists, regard as unanswerable, or at any rate take no interest in answering, the question what we mean by a word in any sense in which this can be distinguished from the empirical criteria on account of which the word is applied. It is therefore fair to say that there has been a great deal of confusion about the matter, and that it is highly probable that most people who put forward naturalist definitions of "good" either never meant at all by "definition" what Moore meant in *Principia Ethica*, or at least confused it with other senses of "definition."

(5) It seems very unsatisfactory to conclude a long ethical discussion with the tame remark that the central concept which we have been discussing cannot be defined. But it is important to realize that to say this is not necessarily to exclude the possibility of being able to say more about it, but only to exclude the possibility of reducing the central concepts of ethics to non-ethical terms. It may be perhaps that, when we have said that they cannot be thus reduced, we shall still be able to say other things of a more positive kind about them, such as that what is good is always the fulfilment of a teleological tendency, or would be desired by all men if they really knew what it was like, or that God commands us to do what we ought. All I am denying is that such statements could exhaust the meaning of the terms "good" or "ought." Even if they are correct descriptions, they are not definitions, at least in the sense under discussion. In that sense some terms must be indefinable, for analysis implies the unanalysable. Those who say that everything can be defined must either be

using "define" in a different sense or be muddled, for every concept could not be reduced without residuum to others. If so, there would be no concepts left at all. But to say that a term is indefinable is not to say that we do not know what it means. It is only to say that the concept for which it stands, with which we may still be perfectly familiar, is too ultimate and unique to be analysed in terms of anything else. I do not indeed hold that "good" is indefinable, for Moore's arguments only support the view that "good" cannot be defined adequately by means of non-ethical terms. But the remarks here will still be relevant to my position, for even if "good" is defined by means of ethical terms, this will still presuppose the indefinability of some ethical term.

(6) Even philosophers who have insisted on analysis have rarely clearly committed themselves to the view that, when they put forward an analysis, they are just giving an account of what people mean in the ordinary sense of "meaning." What they seem often to be doing is rather giving that element in the meaning of a general statement which they take to be true, while rejecting the rest as false, ungrounded, or confused, or, alternatively, stating a proposition which they think has the same implications as the original one. We need not, therefore, be very surprised at the disagreement between the naturalists and the non-naturalists, since the people who disagree with each other are generally trying to do different things. And prior to this century the question whether a naturalist definition was possible or not was hardly ever clearly raised, so that we need not be surprised that it obtained no clear answer.

(7) I do not, indeed, altogether rule out the possibility of a failure to see what might have been discovered by careful attention to what we mean. A circumstance that makes it easier for people to overlook the specifically ethical element which cannot be analysed in terms of psychology is that the

times when we actually have first-hand ethical experience and the times when we discuss philosophically the analysis of good do not usually coincide. It is perhaps even impossible to engage in the two activities exactly simultaneously, so that we are dependent for our ethical experiences on memory when we are philosophizing. For we do not have first-hand ethical experience all the time we do what is right and every time we make a judgement about the good, especially when we take the judgements only as examples for a philosophical argument. Some of our judgements as to good and evil, right and wrong are almost parrotlike; some are mere applications of a general rule the truth of which is not intuited, at least at the time, but taken for granted; some involve an insight into the particular case as regards means but presuppose prior judgements as to ends. It is therefore easier than might be expected to go wrong when we investigate these matters philosophically, because we have not before us at the time a genuine ethical experience, and at the very moment when we have such an experience we are too much concerned with it as a practical issue to philosophize about it. This perhaps explains why good and intelligent men could sometimes put forward quite preposterous ethical theories, for example, egoistic hedonism. In any case whether the naturalist or the non-naturalist is right, we must admit error on one side or the other as to what we mean.

Naturalists and subjectivists usually pride themselves on being empiricists, so one would expect them to base their views mainly on a direct observation of the ethical experience. That this is not their method is to my mind highly significant and should give pause to any would-be converts to their views. Their method is rather to assume on epistemological grounds that any non-naturalist account is almost certainly wrong, and then to try to devise a theory which will come only as close to accepting the empirical evidence as can be done without contradicting this assumption. I prefer to base my account primarily on an examination of my psychological attitude when I consider actual concrete ethical questions. For it is this attitude of which we should be giving an account when we analyse commonsense ethical propositions.

Let us now examine critically the objections to the view that the fundamental concept (or concepts) of ethics is (are) indefinable. Some people are dissatisfied with the view that "good" is indefinable because they want to be able to say more about it than this, and they would probably be dissatisfied for the same reason if "ought" were declared to be indefinable; but we must distinguish between saying more about ethical concepts and reducing all ethical concepts to non-ethical. The indefinability theory need only be a statement that the latter reduction cannot be achieved, leaving it open to make whatever other positive statements about ethical terms we think to be true. Again, Moore's comparison of good and yellow has given rise to misunderstandings. Moore says that good is like yellow in being simple, unanalysable, and discoverable by immediate awareness; he does not suggest that it is like yellow in any other respect. Yellowness is a sensible quality, or rather a class of slightly varying sensible qualities, good a categorial property, but they still might have the features mentioned in common.

Field [4] objected to Moore's account that, whereas it is admittedly an essential feature of goodness that it is capable of moving us to action, the alleged simple indefinable quality has no necessary connection with desire, and cognition without desire cannot move to action. But no doubt Moore would reply that we can see no *reason* in the nature of anything why it arouses desire, but must accept this as an empirical fact, as with all the other inductive generalizations we make, and if

---

[4] *Moral Theory*, pp. 56 ff. I think Field would now admit that his argument referred to a different sense of "definition" from that used by Moore.

so we need not be troubled because we cannot see *a priori* why goodness does stimulate desire.

Then there is the general objection to any concepts supposed not to be derived from mere empirical observation. It is a common assumption that there cannot be any such, but I do not see any conceivable way in which the truth of the assumption might be proved. Indeed I cannot think of any attempt at a proof, unless we are to regard as one the vicious circle of Hume. The latter first concludes that there are, with what he dismisses as an insignificant exception, no ideas derived from impressions, simply because we cannot cite any examples of such.[5] Since he, and not his opponents, wrote the *Treatise*, no examples are of course cited in this passage; but some chapters later when he comes to discuss substance and objective causal connection, which were generally cited as cases of ideas not derived from impressions, he dogmatically denies that we have any such ideas on the ground that they cannot be derived from impressions, a generalization which was only established by ignoring these cases. Any proof that there were no such ideas would in fact already presuppose that there was at least one. For, if the proof were valid, its premises would have to entail its conclusion, and this idea of entailment or necessary logical connection is one that could not be given in mere observation. Whatever non-empirical ideas we may get rid of, we cannot get rid of entailment if we are to have any inference at all. We must therefore decide in each case on its own merits whether an idea is non-empirical or not, since we cannot disprove the possibility of non-empirical ideas by a general argument, and have to admit at least one.

No doubt in one sense ethical ideas are empirical, because even in Moore's theory we could not have any idea what good was if we had never had the experience of apprehending the

---

[5] *Treatise of Human Nature*, I, 1, 1.

property of goodness; but the idea may still be called non-empirical if by this is meant that it is not apprehended by sense perception or by introspection,[*] as I can discover by introspection whether I am angry or feel hot. The same applies to obligation. That they are not apprehended in such a way is surely shown by the fact that, when we see that something is intrinsically good or some act morally obligatory, we also see that it must be so—its factual properties being what they are. Goodness, badness, obligatoriness and wrongness are not properties that could possibly be removed from an experience or action without the experience or action being in other ways different, and this impossibility is not merely the effect of causal laws. Hitler could not have done the actions which had the factual properties his actions towards the Jews possessed and yet have prevented the actions having the additional properties of badness and wrongness. It is not that we generalize from experience that he could not do this, but that the very suggestion is absurd. On the other hand, what we learn by observation might always have been different, at least for anything we can see. This of itself is a strong argument against any view which analyses ethical concepts in terms of the attitude of the person or persons judging. For it is quite conceivable that the attitude of the latter towards the same action might in a particular case have been different from what it actually was so that they disapproved of the action instead of approving of it or vice versa, yet granted that the action had the factual characteristics which it did have it could not

---

[*] This may seem indeed to contradict what I said earlier when I repeatedly based my account on introspection of my ethical attitudes, but it does not really do so. There is no more contradiction in saying that I can discover by introspection that I have an ethical concept which is not itself derived from introspection than there is in saying that I can discover by introspection that I have concepts of physical objects. The apprehension that this concept applied to something would not be itself an act of introspection, but it might still be observable by introspection, as are many psychological phenomena which are not themselves introspections.

have had different ethical characteristics. "Good" cannot mean, for example, "approved," for anything which is good could not, being what it was in other respects, have failed to be good, but it might well, the psychology of the person or persons who make the judgement having been different, a quite contingent circumstance, have not been approved.

I am not suggesting that the fundamental concepts of ethics are innate in any other sense except that we have an innate capacity to apprehend them, and that is only a tautology since whatever we do apprehend we must have a capacity to apprehend. If the characteristics of obligatoriness or goodness belong to any actions or experiences, they and their opposites may be apprehended directly as belonging to the real, for our actions and experiences are just as real as physical objects; and in that case "good" and "ought" are no more innate ideas than are the qualities we discover in sense perception. We could not perceive even the latter if we had not an innate capacity for sense perception. Having apprehended the ethical properties in some actual instances we have the idea of them and may apply it hypothetically even to what is not in existence, since we can see it to follow from the nature of certain things that if they existed they would be good (or, in other cases, bad).

But probably the chief motive which leads people to give a naturalist analysis of ethical propositions is the belief that, if they adopted any other analysis, it would make it impossible to hold any justifiable ethical beliefs, just as the chief motive for adopting a phenomenalist analysis of physical object propositions is the belief that only in this sense can physical object propositions be justified. In both cases it is thought incredible that our commonsense judgements could be quite unjustified, in both it is held that they would be unjustified if interpreted in the *prima facie* more plausible way, and it is therefore concluded that they must be interpreted in another way. Now there might be something in the contention if there were some other positive argument which showed that ethical judgements, if non-naturalistically interpreted, could not be true; but we have seen that such arguments are not available. The worst we could say is that there is a lack of positive justification for non-naturalist ethical propositions, and if so it can be shown that the above argument can provide no support for its conclusion. For there are two premises: one (a) is that, if our ethical propositions are to be interpreted non-naturalistically, we can have no justification for asserting any of them to be true; the other (b) is that we are justified in asserting some ethical propositions to be true. Obviously (b) is needed if (a) is to provide a reason for giving a naturalist analysis of the propositions. By itself, (a) would lead to the conclusion, not that our ethical judgements are to be naturalistically interpreted, but only that, if and in so far as they assert anything which cannot be naturalistically interpreted, we are not justified in saying they are true. But either (b) can be known or rationally believed without first presupposing that the ethical propositions are to be analysed naturalistically or it cannot. If it can (a) is false; if it cannot, there is a vicious circle, because then the second premise presupposes the conclusion. This does not prove that the naturalist analysis is wrong, but it does seem to remove what has been probably the most strongly felt argument for such an analysis.

. Another influential type of argument for naturalism is that we can explain the origin of ethical ideas and beliefs psychologically from the non-ethical. But, even if they originated from non-ethical factors such as, for example, the fear of punishment, this would not prove that they now contained nothing beyond these. If the psychological theory of the origin of ethical ideas merely tells us what experiences preceded their formation, it is innocuous; but if it claims to analyse the ideas in terms of these non-ethical experiences it is open to the objections which I have brought against naturalism.

Further, we are less likely to be wrong about what we mean now than we are to be about the psychological history of the origin of the ideas in children and savages, and we must not reject the more certain for the sake of the less certain. The impossibility of obtaining reliable introspective information must make the psychology of children and savages, at least when we are concerned with anything but simple sense perceptions, highly speculative. The same remark applies to any theory of ethics based on a study of the way in which children learn the use of ethical words.

What is it that is missing from any naturalist or subjectivist account of ethics? Well, I should not like to say the only missing element, but at any rate the most important one is represented by the term "ought." "Good" in its non-natural sense or senses carries with it the notion that the good thing *ought* not to be wantonly sacrificed but, other things being equal, pursued. Now to say that I wish for something or that I have a certain kind of emotional feeling about it, or to exclaim in a way which expresses these psychological states, if that can be distinguished from saying I have them, does not entail that I am under any obligation whatever to produce the objects of this wish or emotion even if I am quite able to and there is no objection to doing so. Nor does the notion of being commanded (or of commanding myself) involve in any way that of being under an obligation unless we presuppose such propositions as that the person who commands has a special claim on me such that I ought to obey him, or that the action commanded is on its own account my duty apart from the fact of its being commanded, and to presuppose these propositions is already to assume the fact of obligation. Similarly, that everybody or most people or some group of people will feel an emotion of approval towards me if I do x may make me more inclined to do x because I like this result, but it is quite incapable of putting me under an obligation to do x. As Kant insisted, we can see that the "ought" is quite distinct from the "is," and this is fatal to all naturalist definitions. "Ought" is what subjectivist and naturalist theories leave out, and to have an ethics without "ought" is like playing Hamlet without the Prince of Denmark. The stand against naturalism has usually been made in relation to the notion of "good," but to make it in relation to "ought" would have been to take up an even securer line of defence. Only, if once it is granted that we cannot give a naturalist or subjectivist account of "ought," it is then in any case unreasonable to try to give one of all senses of "good." For it is plain that at least some meanings of good, for example, morally good, include a reference to the non-naturalist ought.

Of course a naturalist might claim to analyse moral obligation in terms of approval or desire, but it is even more plain that to say to A that he ought not to cheat B is not merely to make a statement about his or other people's psychology than is the corresponding proposition in the case of "good" or "bad." There is surely some concept there quite different from that of any psychological feeling or empirical tendency? The concept carries with it a unique authority which does not belong to any other feeling or desire as such and is quite irrespective of whether it happens to be in accord with the keenest or most widespread feeling or the strongest or most widely influential desire. "That principle by which we survey, and either approve or disapprove our own heart, temper, and actions, is not only to be considered as what is in its turn to have some influence, which may be said of every passion, of the lowest appetites; but likewise as being superior, as from its very nature manifestly claiming superiority over all others, insomuch that you cannot form a notion of this faculty conscience, without taking in judgement, direction, superintendency . . . Had it strength as it has right, had it power as it has manifest authority, it would absolutely govern the world." [7]

It will be noticed that I have so far not tried to refute the particular naturalist theories one by one but have claimed that we can see at once that any naturalist theory must be wrong.[8] That we should be able to perceive such a truth as that "good" and "ought" are not definable in purely psychological terms need not occasion surprise any more than the fact that we can perceive it to be true that sights cannot be reduced to sounds. Even a naturalist would presumably admit that he can see that goodness or obligation is not analysable in terms of numbers and would not say, "Well, I have tried various definitions of 'good' in terms of numbers, $3 + 4$, $5 + 7$, $6 + 9$ etc., and have not found any which would fit, but perhaps somebody will some day find one which does." No, he would see that it was ridiculous to suppose this could ever happen, because numbers and ethical properties are fundamentally discrepant in their natures so that one can never be reduced to the other. I should claim that, if we once grasp the issue clearly and keep it steadily before our minds, we can see the same about psychological definitions of ethical concepts or definitions of them in terms of any other science. I do not therefore think it necessary to consider separately the various naturalist definitions that have been proposed, but perhaps if I do so briefly it will bring out my points still more clearly.

The view that "good" means "approved by me" I have already considered under the heading of subjectivism, but it has sometimes been held that "good" or "right" means "approved by most people" or "approved by the society in which I live." The theory might also be expressed by saying that

---

[7] Butler, *Sermon* II, § 19.
[8] I think we can perceive directly that good is not analysable in psychological terms, but not that it is simple.

"goodness" means "the power to arouse the emotion of approval." I do not see how such a view is to escape the obvious criticism that a conscientious objector or a martyr might without contradicting himself hold both that something was bad or wrong and that it was approved by most people in his society or in the world. Whether he judged rightly in the particular case or not is irrelevant: right or wrong, he is certainly not committing a verbal contradiction. Again, if we defined "good" or "right" as "approved by people in general," and not only in a particular society, an insuperable difficulty would arise about what constituted a majority. If we took into account everybody who ever lived—and I do not see where we can consistently stop short of this—we should arrive at some queer results for, taking into account all past ages, very crude and savage far outnumber even partially civilized men. If, on the other hand, we redress the balance by including all the men who ever will live, it becomes quite impossible to decide what the majority will approve. If we say that "good" or "right" means "approved by the social group of the speaker," we shall have to admit that the Nazis spoke truly when they said that it was right to ill-treat the Jews. It might be suggested that "good" or "right" always meant "approved by some group which the speaker had in mind," but that the group might vary with the context and speaker. But this would make the meaning of ethical statements shift in an impossible fashion. The Nazi who said it was right to send Jews to concentration camps would on that view still be saying what was true, for most members of the social group he had in mind felt approval for the action. In saying it was wrong I should also be speaking the truth; but that is not good enough. When I say it is wrong I am claiming that the Nazi is mistaken even if the social group he had in mind felt approval of the action; I am not merely saying that, though in his sense of the word he was right, in mine he was wrong.

On this view there would be no sense in saying any group was right rather than any other, unless it was merely meant that the group of the speaker felt more approval for that group than for the other. And if I could only influence my group so as to change their feelings and make them approve, anything I did would be right, whatever it was. It should also be noted that most of the ethical judgements we make are about particular actions, states of mind, characters, which are not generally known, so that on the approval theory the judgement "This is good" or "right" must mean, not that a majority actually approve this, but that they would approve it if they knew about it. This seems to me to make the view still less plausible. Surely ethical judgements about what has been actually done claim to assert an actual fact, not what only would be a fact if something else happened which we know will never happen, that is, if most people were to know of the particular actions or states of mind in myself, perhaps secret, perhaps known just to a few people, which I approve or condemn. And surely ethical judgements are judgements about the action etc. named in them, not about something quite different, that is, the feelings of other people, still less about something that does not exist, that is, the feelings most people would have if they knew of the action, which they do not.

Again, as I have pointed out earlier, it is plain that whether something is good or right is not a question that could be settled straight off merely by disclosing a set of statistics, if we had them, about people's feelings. For instance, if it were discovered that the feeling of approval of most people towards something was always in strict proportion to the amount of pleasure they thought it produced and depended solely on that, it would by no means follow necessarily that hedonism was the true theory of ethics. We should not alter our ethical opinions as to the goodness or badness of something or the rightness or wrongness of some act straightway as a matter of course just because we found that the majority of people had different feelings from ourselves about it. Such a discovery would indeed be liable to influence us, but it would be ridiculous to say that it would necessarily be or ought to be the only deciding factor, as should be the case on the approval view. Again, the degree of approval or disapproval felt varies in proportion to circumstances which are admittedly irrelevant to the ethical quality of its object. For instance, men tend to feel more approval for the acts of close friends than for those of enemies or even strangers. It is difficult to see how the impartiality necessary for ethics is to be given a place in such a theory. The objection might be met by analysing "A is right" or "A is good" as meaning "most men feel approval of A in so far as they are not affected by irrelevant circumstances," but I do not see how "irrelevant" could be defined without circularity. It can only mean "what is irrelevant to the rightness or goodness of A." It will not do to define "influenced by irrelevant circumstances" as meaning "feeling in a way in which you would not feel if you were not personally affected," for example, because it is *you* whose interests have been injured, for this does not cover all cases of irrelevancy. If I felt more disapproval of a man's deeds just because he was a Jew I should be affected by irrelevant circumstances, even where his acts did not concern me personally at all. The majority of men are less inclined to feel approval of the actions of somebody if the latter is unattractive in appearance and in superficial matters unconventional. Does it follow that physically unattractive and unconventional men are morally worse than others? Further, the belief that other people approve or disapprove what I propose to do owes more than half its effect on me to the belief that their emotions would be objectively justified, that there are qualities in my proposed action which would make it fitting to approve or disapprove it.

Finally, the notion of obligation is neither contained in the notion of general approval nor deducible from it. On the contrary it is an essential feature of the moral consciousness that I realize that, if I ought to do something, I ought to do it whether others feel approval of it or not. Obligation need not, indeed, conflict with the approval of others, and their approval may even be one of the factors in helping to determine what I am under an obligation to do, since—other things being equal—I am more likely to do good by doing what is generally approved than by doing what is not so approved. But if "what ought to be done" means "what is generally approved," general approval would have to be the only factor which ultimately counted in deciding what we ought to do, and this it certainly is not. We can even say that indifference to approval is an essential part of the notion of obligation, because once we grant that something is our duty it follows that we ought to do it irrespective of whether others feel approval or not. Their approval is a contingent accident. This point may be made clearer still by considerations such as the following: It is obvious that we ought to seek what is good and/or right as the only end in itself. But it certainly is not the case that we ought to seek what other people approve as the only end-in-itself or even a main end-in-itself just because they feel approval of it. And I cannot see what point there could possibly be in doing what other people would approve *if* they knew what I have done when in fact they do not know it, unless there is some other reason besides the approval; yet, if something is my duty, I clearly ought to do it whether other people know of it or not. The good man will not value approval except as a sign of something objectively right or good. Views that ethical predicates are to be defined in terms of the commands of society or combinations of this with approval theories are open to similar objections.

Perhaps a little less unplausible are the naturalist theories which try to define "good" in terms of desire. It might be held that "good" meant either what somebody desires or what the speaker desires or what most people desire. These views might also be expressed by saying that "goodness" equals "the power to arouse desire." It has been objected that you can desire only what is absent, while the good may be present. But I think this objection could be met, without fundamentally altering what the holders of these theories maintain, by substituting "desired or liked" for "desired." Desire and liking are, I think, fundamentally the same attitude except that desire has for its object what is absent and liking what is present. If "good" is defined in terms of desire or liking, "the right action" or "the action we ought to do" will probably be defined as the one most efficient as a means to the fulfilment of desires or to the production of what is liked. The objection that it is not by any means self-contradictory to say that an action is not the most efficient means to this and yet that we ought to do it seems to me adequate to refute this view of "right," whichever form of the desire theory we take. For instance, Kant or Ross would say that we ought to keep certain promises even if we were convinced that alternative actions more efficient as means towards the fulfilment of desires or the production of what was liked were open to us, and nobody has claimed that their view is self-contradictory, though many have said it was false. Somebody might also combine a desire theory of good with an approval theory of right, but this would subject him both to the objections against approval theories and the objections against desire theories, and so it need not be discussed. I cannot see what other naturalist theory of "right" could be plausibly combined with the desire theory of good, and the objections to these theories of "right" are therefore for me objections against the desire theory of good.

The first form of the desire theory, that "good" means "desired by somebody," is adopted by R. B. Perry, except that he substitutes for desire the term "interest," which also covers liking. Now is this view not obviously false, since people desire and like bad things? It will be retorted that, if something is desired or liked, it must be in one aspect good, and will be desired for that aspect, though it may still be wrong to seek it, because that aspect is outweighed by its bad aspects or by the evil means necessary to obtain it. But it is not easy to apply this to people who desire the torture of others or even to less desperately wicked desires "to have one's own back," for what seems to be desired here is the pain of the other man, and not only, or perhaps at all, the advantages which the pain is conceived to bring. To reply that it is not his pain but one's own pleasure in the pain that is desired seems to me to be a case of the hedonistic fallacy. A man would not take pleasure in revenge if he did not desire revenge as an end-in-itself and not merely as a means. Further, it would certainly not be self-contradictory to say both that somebody desires A and that A is intrinsically and wholly evil, whether such a thing ever occurs in fact or not. In the second place, if "good" means desired, what does "better" mean? Could it in that case possibly mean anything else but "more desired" or "desired by more people"? This would commit one to the view that not only are desire, liking, and interest always directed to what is good, but that desire, liking, and interest are in exact proportion to the goodness of their objects, if not in the individual, at any rate when we take into account the desires of different people. This is surely a fantastic hypothesis which has no ground whatever. If we are considering the desires of people in general, it is obvious that on the whole (though with considerable exceptions) riches and what they bring, for instance, have been desired and liked in excess of their real value. Further, as with all these other naturalist definitions, even if the proposition that things were desired or liked in proportion to their real value were true, it would express not a tautology but a contingent fact or at the most a universal causal law of psychology.

The second view, that "good" means "desired (or liked) by the speaker," falls under the heading of subjectivist views, but the criticisms which I have just brought against a corresponding naturalist view in the last paragraph can be turned also against it, besides the special objection that it would commit us to a completely egoist view of good.

The view that "good" means "what most people desire (or like)" is open to similar objections. Most people desire and like happiness more than great virtue, yet it does not therefore necessarily follow that the former is better. And, if we could count heads, we should no doubt find that the majority of people who have hitherto lived, which would of course include a great preponderance of the "uncivilized," desired revenge on those who they thought had wronged them and did not desire to forgive these. Is revenge therefore good and forgiveness bad? In any case it is surely obvious that no collection of statistics as to people's desires would of itself completely settle the question what is good. Still less could a vague statement about such statistics, for example, that more than fifty per cent (or eighty per cent) of people desired or liked so-and-so, be possibly regarded as equivalent to the statement that so-and-so was good. All three theories would encounter extreme difficulties in defining "better" in terms of "desired or liked more." Even if action be the criterion of desire, it is certainly not, in view of the frequency of wrong and bad actions, the criterion of rightness or goodness. The definition of "better" could not be in terms of felt intensity of desire, because this varies according to many quite irrelevant circumstances, for example, mood or proximity in time of expected satisfaction, to say nothing of bad desires. If, on the other hand, we say either that the measure of the strength of a desire, at least for this purpose, should be taken to be not its felt strength as a desire but the degree of satisfaction which will accrue when it is fulfilled, or frankly define "good" as "satisfaction of desire" or "what satisfies desire," this is equally difficult to measure, even apart from the difficulty of making predictions about it.[9] If the measure is to be felt intensity and duration of satisfaction we are virtually committed to a hedonistic theory of ethics, and hedonism as a definition of "good" is even less plausible than hedonism as a theory of what things are good. Permanence of satisfaction is often suggested as a criterion, but it is just as inadequate to measure only the duration, and ignore the intensity, as vice versa. Or, it is said, good is what satisfies the whole man. But this is not true if by "satisfying the whole man" is meant "satisfying all his desires." It does not satisfy his wrong desires, and since no man can live a good life without sacrificing even some satisfactions innocent in themselves it will not satisfy even all his good and justified desires. If we say that the unsatisfied desires will eventually disappear and that the whole man will then be satisfied, we are open to the objection that many of the better desires, if unsatisfied, would likewise disappear, perhaps more quickly. It is a commonplace that one of the evil effects of persistently following the lower rather than the higher is that it destroys desire for the higher. This might happen, not only in an individual, but in a whole race who neglected culture and liberal education. We cannot meet this objection simply by arguing that such an individual or race would enjoy less pleasure and suffer more pain, because this is just to fall back on hedonism. We could only meet it by drawing a distinction as regards importance and quality between the different parts of one's nature sacrificed or their satisfaction, and I do not see how this could be worked out except on the basis of the belief that some factors in our nature or experience were qualitatively better than others in a non-

---

[9] On this subject v. W. D. Ross, *International Journal of Ethics*, XXXVII, p. 117 ff.

natural sense of "better." To define "good" as "that which satisfies the more important parts of our nature," or as "what we desire in so far as we are influenced only by relevant considerations," is to commit a vicious circle, since "more important" here can only mean "intrinsically or instrumentally better," and "relevant" can only mean "such as to affect its goodness."

All forms of the desire theory are clearly open to the fundamental objections which hold against any naturalist view of good. (1) To say that what is desired, whether by anyone or by oneself or by most people, or what satisfies desires in the long run, is good is not to assert a verbal proposition which cannot be denied without self-contradiction. (2) No collection of statistics as to people's desires or their satisfactions could settle the question what was good. (3) You cannot derive obligation from desire. Indeed it seems to me that to obtain what one desires is good only because of the specific quality of the object desired, or because pleasure in general is good and the fulfilment of desire brings pleasure. If the reference is to one's own desires, it seems plain that, so far from obligation being derivable from these, we are conscious of obligation primarily in independence from or even opposition to what we most keenly desire. If it is meant that we ought to do what will satisfy people's desires in general and not only our own, I do not see what *locus standi* the naturalist who holds this position can have against the person who asks, "Why ever should I bother about other people's desires (except in so far as to do so is a means to satisfying my own)?" This question could be answered only by admitting that it is obligatory for us to try to satisfy them, in some sense of "obligatory" which does not itself mean merely "conducive to the satisfaction of desire." If the naturalist then admits this and gives some other naturalist definition of "obligatory," for example, in terms of approval, the question may be asked again: "Why on earth should a man bother about gaining the approval of most people unless he wants to do so more than he wants to perform an action which would forfeit their approval?" The naturalist view to my mind takes all the point away from morality.

A slightly different view would be that to call anything "good" is to say that it is the object of some "pro attitude" on the part of most people. Following Ross I use "pro attitude" to cover desiring, liking, seeking, choosing, approving, admiring, etc. These attitudes obviously have something in common which is suitably indicated by the prefix *pro-*. Such a view would be more elastic and has a considerable affinity to the definition which I shall finally adopt, but it is obviously still exposed to the main objections brought against the approval and desire theories. It is perfectly sensible to say that something is bad or wrong though most people have a pro attitude to it, and the pro attitude of others carries with it no obligation on me except in so far as I already presuppose that it is good for them that their desires should be fulfilled. In fact if the reader cared to run through the last few pages again he would find that the theory in question was liable to most of the objections brought against either the approval or the desire theory. It should be noted that in working the theory out we can only include "approve" under the pro attitudes in the uncommon sense in which it signifies "have a certain emotion towards," not in the sense in which it signifies "think right" (or "good"). If we defined "right" or "good" in terms of "approve" in the latter sense, we should be defining it in terms of itself.

In view of the fact that people desire many things which they would not desire if they knew what they really involved, it has been suggested that "good" means, not what is actually desired, but what all men would desire if they knew its true nature; but such a view is open to many objections. It is still naturalist in character and therefore open to the general objections which we have brought against all naturalist views, besides some peculiar to itself. The terms used in the definition are purely psychological, and the fact that the property identified with goodness is hypothetical and not categorical does not make any essential difference. We still cannot derive an ought from mere psychological facts about desire, or if we could it would certainly be a synthetic and not an analytic proposition, so that we should still have at least one ethical concept irreducible to psychological terms, namely, the concept signified by "ought." That all men would desire whatever is good in proportion to its goodness if only they knew its true nature is a highly doubtful proposition, so far from being merely verbal, and I see no means of proving it or even showing it to be at all probable. For us to desire the good of all other men fully as much as an equivalent amount of good for ourselves or those closest to us it would be necessary not only that we should know all the circumstances including the state of their feelings, but that our emotional nature should be completely altered. And, if we imagine our emotional nature thus completely and superhumanly or inhumanly altered, we can no longer have any foundation for saying what we should desire under the circumstances. In any case it is surely obvious that to call anything good is not to say what would happen if some quite impossible psychological revolution were effected in our nature. But, even if it were a fact that we are so built that we should desire what was good in proportion to its goodness if we knew its true nature, it would be a quite contingent fact, for we still might well have been built differently. Further, we are sometimes immediately aware that something is good or bad, but hypothetical facts about what would happen if our situation and nature were quite different from what it is are not facts that any philosopher in any other context has ever suggested could be known immediately. How could we know by intuition the truth of such extraordinary prophecies?

Some would-be naturalists admit that we can see any naturalist analysis to be incomplete, but attempt to meet the objection by calling in subjectivism as an ally and contending that naturalist definitions leave out something, but only the emotional or hortatory element. In that case an "ethical judgement" is really a psychological judgement plus an exclamation, wish, or command. "You are acting wrongly" becomes, for example, "You are interfering with the fulfilment of other people's desires, damn you!" or "You are deceiving people; stop doing this." But this is to make the worst of both worlds. For the position is liable to the main criticisms already brought against subjectivist modes of analysis, since it involves a subjectivist view not indeed of the whole judgement but of the only specifically ethical part. And it does not in any case escape the main objections against naturalism, for it is just as obvious that the element in "ethical judgements" which is capable of being true or false includes more than can be given in any naturalist analysis as it is that the "judgement" as a whole does so. The view I am criticizing tries to avoid the objections to subjectivism by admitting an assertive element in "ethical judgements" but denying that it is non-naturalistic, and the objections to naturalism by admitting an element which is not merely an assertion about human psychology but denying that it is assertive at all. I reply that my objections, if valid, show that there is an *assertive* element in ethical judgements which is *non-naturalistic*, and I can therefore claim them to be just as valid against this combination of subjectivism and naturalism as against either view undiluted by the other.

Again, some naturalists try to escape objections by shifting the meaning of "good." When objections to a particular view of "good" are pointed out, they say that, while this view applies to some uses of "good," in the cases where objection is taken "good" is being used in a different sense, though one that is still naturalist or subjectivist. If objections are brought against this second sense, they can then say in any case where the objections are insuperable that "good" is being used not in this second sense but in the first or in a third sense. They may thus hope that, whatever particular objection is brought, they can always find some sense of "good" which will avoid this particular objection, and that the other objections to which the new definition may be liable will apply only in cases where they could claim that "good" was being used in another sense without exposing themselves to worse objections. For example, if "good" or "right" is defined as that of which most men feel approval and it is then pointed out that a moral reformer or conscientious objector may, without contradicting himself, assert that something is bad or wrong while admitting that most people feel approval of it, the naturalist may try to avoid the difficulty by saying that "good" or "right" as used by him in this context means not "what most men approve" but "what I, the speaker, approve." If then it is objected, for example, that in that case two men do not contradict each other when one asserts that A is bad and the other that A is good, he may retort that, in cases where they do really contradict each other, they are using "good" not in the second sense but in the first or in some third sense, for instance, as meaning what will satisfy most men's desires in the long run. But it seems plain to me that the main objections I feel about any exclusively naturalist or subjectivist analysis apply to all such attempts at analysis and cannot therefore be avoided by putting forward one analysis in one case and another in another case. I have admitted [10] that there are some senses of "good"—not ethical ones—which have to be analysed naturalistically; but I claim to have given adequate reason for

---

[10] V. above, p. 46.

thinking that there are some others which cannot be analysed in any naturalist or subjectivist way at all, not only that each of the particular attempts made at such analysis fails to do justice to some of the senses of "good." When I use a sentence such as commonly expresses an "ethical judgement," not parrotlike but sincerely and with clear consciousness of what I am doing, it is quite clear to me that I am asserting something which may be either true or false (except in so far as I think I see it to be certainly true and therefore cannot entertain the idea of its being false), and which is not merely about my state of mind or disposition, thus excluding any subjectivist analysis. It is also quite clear to me that I am asserting something which goes beyond any statement about people's psychology, thus excluding naturalism. The chief objections that I have brought against subjectivist modes of analysis apply equally to any or all of them, and the chief objections that I have brought against naturalism apply equally to all forms of naturalism. The same insight shows the falsity of all; and it seems perfectly clear to me that, if other people mean at all the same sort of thing when they use ethical words as I do (which assumption, though not strictly provable, is most unlikely to be wrong), no subjectivist or naturalist can possibly give an adequate analysis of what they mean. No doubt there are some objections applying only to particular forms of either theory which might be avoided by shifting the meaning. But each time the naturalist has to save himself by postulating a shift of meaning where there is no other reason for supposing this except to bolster up naturalism, the plausibility of his case is lessened, and he will have to do it very often. No doubt "good" and "ought" are used in various different senses, but this does not justify us in assuming a different sense just to fit in with a preconceived theory in cases where we should otherwise never have supposed such a thing. If in defining a term we are to be allowed, whenever our theory of its definition does not fit, to say "Oh, the speaker must be using the term in a different sense"—and then do the same again about the second sense, we shall be able to defend some very odd definitions. In defining we surely must not suppose a difference of usage unless there is evidence for it to be found in a direct study of the proposition asserted and its context, and not do so merely in order to save a general theory about the definition. Such a theory should be based on a study of general usage taking into account its differences and not serve as a premise for inferring differences which would otherwise never have occurred to us.

Merely biological definitions of fundamental ethical concepts would be still harder to defend.[11] "Good" or "right" cannot just mean "what tends to further human survival," for in ethics we aim at the good life as well as at mere life, and though some virtues and vices are likely to affect the duration of life or the number of descendants produced this is not the case with most. If the view mentioned were adopted it would follow logically that one of the worst crimes was to remain a childless bachelor, and that it did not matter how miserable one made anybody else provided the misery did not actually shorten his life or diminish the chance of his having many descendants! If we try a sociological definition and substitute for mere survival the survival of the existing type of society, this would rule out all very radical reforms as necessarily unethical. If we say that "good or right is what furthers the evolution of society," we are faced with the difficulty of defining evolution and distinguishing it from other kinds of change without already presupposing the notion of goodness. There can be no chance of defining "good" in terms of evolution, unless, as is often the case, we mean by "evolution"

---

[11] For criticism of a biological view of ethics that has come to the front lately, that is, that of C. H. Waddington, see Ewing in *Proceedings of Aristotelian Soc.*, XLII, 68 ff and Broad, *id.*, pp. 100 A ff.

"good change," and that would constitute a vicious circle. For all development is not necessarily good, whether "development" just means change or whether it is defined in terms of increased complexity. It is not even an obviously true, let alone verbal, proposition that change going further in the same direction as that which it has predominantly followed in the past is good. There are times when it is best to make a sharp turn and, having developed a certain mode of action up to a point, adopt a quite different one, and this may be true of the race as well as of the individual. For instance one of the features of change in the past has been that people have shown more and more efficiency in destroying each other in war. Does it follow that it would be good for this process to continue? If it is said in reply that this is not a fundamental enough development to figure in the criterion, it becomes a matter quite impossible to settle what is and what is not fundamental enough to do so. Besides, we shall then be left with nothing but one or two generalizations far too vague to be capable of application. Finally, the fact that change has developed in a certain way in the past cannot possibly itself entail any proposition about what ought to be done. There is nothing logically absurd about the supposition that the whole evolutionary process was harmful and that it would have been better if life had never developed beyond its first stage, or any intermediate stage we might happen to fancy.

The main objections against naturalist theories of ethics may be summed up as follows:

1. It is clear that ethical propositions cannot be established merely by giving statistics of people's psychological reactions, and still clearer, if possible, that they are not themselves propositions about statistics, as they would have to be if they asserted merely "Most people feel . . ."

2. Whatever empirical property is put forward as a definition of "good" or "obligatory," it is clear that the question

whether everything that is good (or obligatory) has that property or vice versa is not merely a question of definition.

3. If something has the property of goodness or obligatoriness at all, we can see that it must have that property in the degree in which it has it, provided only its factual properties are what they are. Yet it is always conceivable to us that the attitude of people to it, or its relation to their desires, in terms of which "good" or "obligatoriness" has been naturalistically defined might have been different, its other factual properties being what they were. Therefore goodness or obligatoriness cannot be identified with being the object of a certain attitude or standing in a certain relation to desire.

4. The naturalist definitions leave out the essential nature of obligation. If they constituted a full account of the meaning of "ought" and "good" there would be no point in my trying to do what I ought rather than anything else which I happened to desire.

5. When we make ethical judgements about an action or state of mind, we are clearly talking primarily about this action or state of mind, not about other states of mind, still less, states which are purely hypothetical, that is, the feelings or attitudes most people would have towards the action or state of mind if they knew about it, which they usually do not.

6. We can after careful reflection see that ethical concepts are generically different from, and therefore incapable of reduction to, the concepts of psychology or any other empirical science.

It is clear that in none of these cases can the missing element be supplied by subjectivism, that is, by admitting that naturalism cannot give a complete account of ethical propositions but maintaining that what is left out is not something which could be objectively true, but only the expression of an emotion or a command. For, if we look at any of these arguments again, we can see that they show, not merely that any naturalist analysis is incomplete in respect of not including the emotional overtones, but that such an analysis does not do justice to the objective element in the judgement itself, namely that for which truth is claimed. Ethical judgements assert truths which go beyond any psychological or biological statistics; to apply ethical properties to whatever has any psychological or biological property is to make a (not merely verbal) objective assertion and not only to add injunctions or expressions of emotion. The ethical properties ascribed to something, if they belong to it at all, *must* so belong, its intrinsic nature being what it is, whereas the emotional attitude of the speaker as well as of others is contingent. If I am to be under any obligation, it must be objectively true that I am under the obligation, and therefore, if there is no adequate naturalist definition of obligation, the deficiency cannot be supplied by emotions or desires which do not claim truth. Ethical judgements are expressions of belief about what we call their objects, and not merely either expressions of something other than belief or expressions of belief about something else, such as people's states of approval, or both together. Ethical concepts are generically different from the merely psychological concepts which either on the subjectivist or on the naturalist view make up the only elements of which they could be composed. In short, the arguments for the view that a naturalist analysis of ethical judgements must be inadequate are at the same time arguments for the view that such an analysis cannot do justice even to the objective element in these judgements.

If we have thus to admit that "good" and "ought" in their ethical senses stand for non-natural concepts, it is still logically possible to avoid admitting that the non-natural properties thus conceived belong to anything. We may admit that most human beings believe in the truth of ethical propositions in a sense in which these cannot be analysed naturalistically, and yet we may hold that they are mistaken in doing so and that these propositions are true of nothing, or at least that we are not justified in thinking them true of anything. This is the position of the moral sceptic, which I earlier classed as a variety of subjectivism. But I cannot believe that all our ethical beliefs are false or unjustified, and therefore I accept the view that the non-natural properties or relations for which the terms "good" and "ought" stand in some of their usages really belong to some selves, experiences, or actions. It, further, seems to be the case that people have analysed ethical propositions naturalistically or subjectively chiefly because they thought that they could then and only then still go on saying that the ethical propositions were true. If people who think like this realize that no naturalist or subjectivist analysis of ethical propositions can be adequate, it may be that they will prefer to admit the real existence of non-natural ethical properties rather than take up a position of ethical scepticism. This ought to be the case especially with those philosophers who take the view in general that commonsense propositions are true and that it is the business of philosophers to analyse them, for ethical propositions are certainly propositions of common sense. Hence the importance of the question of analysis discussed in this chapter. Those who accept views like mine as to the analysis of ethical propositions but doubt whether these propositions are true of anything are referred to what I said in the first chapter.[12] Those who are influenced by what I say but still think that there is an important element of truth in naturalism are asked to wait till Chapter V, when I shall say what I think that to be.

---

[12] V. above, p. 30 ff.

CHAPTER III

The Coherence Theory of Ethics, and Some Other Non-naturalist Definitions of the Fundamental Ethical Terms

If we reject the naturalist and subjectivist views of ethics, is there any alternative to admitting that the fundamental ethical concept is just indefinable and can be grasped by intuition but not further described? Many find this a very unsatisfactory view. But it may be retorted with point that some concepts *must* be indefinable in the sense of "unanalysable," since you cannot reduce everything by analysis to something else without a vicious circle or infinite regress; and it is surely clear that, if all ethical concepts are analysable completely in terms of non-ethical, this will reduce ethics to something else and destroy its distinctive nature altogether. If, however, ethical terms are not all to be defined (analysed) in terms of non-ethical, since they cannot all be defined in terms of each other, at least one ethical concept must be indefinable. This does not imply that its nature cannot be known—it may be very distinctly known—only that it cannot be reduced to anything else. Nor need it imply that nothing more can be said about it. It may perhaps turn out possible to say a great deal more about it; only what is said will never exhaust its nature without residuum. When he denied that "good" was definable, Moore [1] was using "definition" to cover only definition by analysis. We may use "define

---

[1] In speaking of Moore's views I shall refer to those maintained in *Principia Ethica* and *Ethics*, and not to his present views, which in the absence of fresh published works on Ethics are not known.

A" to mean "give properties which accompany A and constitute a distinguishing mark of the presence of A" or "fix the place of A in the system of concepts"; and in these senses it might be possible to define "good," though the term was in Moore's sense indefinable. Again, it may turn out that "good" can be defined, even in Moore's sense, in terms of other ethical concepts or partly of ethical and partly of psychological concepts; but in any case that would still leave some fundamental ethical term, such as "ought," which could not be thus defined. About the fundamental ethical term we naturally want to be able to say something more than that we know what it means but cannot explain it; yet it is important to insist that it stands for a quite distinctive quality or relation which cannot just be identified with any mere object of psychological introspection or any concept derived merely from the latter source.

Now if we keep strictly to Moore's sense of definition, it seems clear to me that a definition exclusively in metaphysical or logical terms would explain away the distinctive character of ethics just as much as would a definition in terms of psychology. When I say this, however, I do not mean to rule out of court the view that everything which we call good has, besides the attribute of goodness, other attributes which are correlated or perhaps inseparably connected with goodness, and that we may make important philosophical generalizations about the attributes in question. Bearing this in mind let us consider the theory which seeks to define goodness in terms of coherence. We shall, first, consider briefly whether such a definition can be regarded as giving a fully adequate equivalent of goodness; that is, as a definition in Moore's sense. Then, if we answer the first question in the negative, we shall ask whether such a theory, if it does not do this, can still provide a definition in some other sense or at least give us important information about ethical matters.

The most elaborate account of the coherence theory of

ethics that I know is given in Professor Paton's book, *The Good Will*, which puts forward the view that to be good is to be coherently willed. Now if this were taken in the way in which the author did not mean it to be taken, that is, as a definition in Moore's sense, it would certainly be very open to criticism. I have indeed heard his view wrongly interpreted as giving one of the naturalist definitions which I have rejected —the definition of "good" as meaning "what will ultimately satisfy us"—on the ground that this alone could be consistently willed, since all wrong doing is due to a search for satisfaction, which yet cannot be obtained by wrong doing.[2] Or, if the egoism implied in such an account is rejected, as I should reject it, and the view is interpreted in terms of general satisfaction, we still have to note that the definition of "good" as what will give satisfaction to somebody (whether oneself or another), or to people in general, is a definition in purely psychological terms and therefore an example of the naturalist error. This is still the case even if we qualify "satisfaction" by a word like "real" or "ultimate," unless we thereby covertly introduce into the definition a non-psychological content.

On the other hand, as Paton maintains while repudiating the view that a thing is made good merely by being willed or desired, it seems at least plausible to say that nothing could be good unless it could satisfy some kind of desire or will. The character and value of the view thus depends on the nature of the predicate introduced to distinguish good willing from the other kinds of willing. Now coherence is certainly a logical and not a psychological concept, and still less is it an object of sense perception. The coherence theory might therefore be less unfairly accused of reducing ethics, not to psychological, but to logical terms, or to a combination of the two. This would exempt it from the charge of naturalism, for the pres-

---

[2] Bosanquet and Bradley both "define" good as "what satisfies," but I cannot think they were then using "define" in the sense of the naturalist.

ence of some naturalist elements in a definition does not make the definition naturalist, unless there are no other elements in it except the naturalist ones. But, if it is intended to give a definition of "good" or "right" in Moore's sense, the coherence theory can in any case fairly be accused of committing the same sort of error as naturalism; that is, of trying to reduce ethics without residuum to the non-ethical. For it is as impossible to get ethical content out of the merely logical as out of the merely psychological, or out of a combination of logical and psychological terms as out of either taken in isolation.

"Coherence" might also be identified with a kind of harmony of different wills together with an internal harmony within the individual's life, such harmony being analogous to, though different from, logical consistency. This brings one nearer to Paton's view, and, if we are to deduce all ethical judgements from a single principle, this is perhaps the most plausible line of derivation; but, if this is intended as a definition in Moore's sense, it will still be naturalist, unless we have already covertly included goodness in the conception of "harmony." "Good" cannot be defined as harmony, at least in Moore's sense, for there is no *verbal* contradiction in saying even that war is intrinsically better, though less harmonious, than peace. Such a definition would confuse the questions what goodness is and what things are good. The considerations that I have brought forward would apply equally to a coherence definition of "right" or "obligation," if one of these terms was taken as fundamental in ethics instead of "good." The same objections hold also against the view that "good" applied to the will means just "aimed at harmony." There is no *verbal* contradiction in saying that a good will might be aimed at lessening harmony instead of increasing it.

But, while these objections may apply to some people who have accepted the coherence theory of ethics, I do not think they would apply to its more distinguished exponents. Professor Paton, for instance, makes it quite clear that he is not providing a definition in Moore's sense of the term. Yet he is not content to say that he is merely giving an account of a quality, coherence, which all good things have over and above the quality of goodness. He admits that to be good and to be coherently willed are not just the same thing; but he insists that the only alternative to saying this is not to say that they are "just two different things each of which is and is knowable in entire isolation from the other." [3] Moore himself does not, however, hold that goodness is separable from the other properties of something good in the sense that goodness could ever fail to be present, the other properties being what they are. He admits that we can rightly make synthetic *a priori* judgements to the effect that, if something has certain qualities, it is necessarily in so far good. But this does not content Paton, who "cannot believe that it is possible to understand thinking on the supposition that some judgements are just analytical and others just synthetic." Paton cannot see how there can be synthetic *a priori* judgements connecting other properties with goodness, if goodness is just simple and quite intelligible apart from its relations; and I for my part am inclined to agree that this is difficult to understand. I do not wish to discuss the question whether Paton has given an adequate interpretation of Moore, but the latter's account certainly does seem to imply that once we have apprehended goodness by a kind of intuition we have apprehended all there is in it!

The holders of the coherence theory do not mean to maintain that all *a priori* propositions are analytic in the sense of verbal. Indeed there is no view more opposed to their conception of the *a priori* than that one; but they would say that, where what is called a synthetic *a priori* proposition con-

---

[3] *The Good Will*, p. 52.

necting A and B is true, neither A nor B could be understood without reference to the other, so that each would have no complete nature by itself, whether definable or indefinable, independently of the other.

We might, I think, combine the essential truth in both views, if we realize that it may be the case that a property is not just reducible to other properties and yet that it may be intrinsically impossible to see what it is like apart from them. "Four" does not just mean two plus two, since it also is six minus two, and the square root of sixteen, etc.; but we cannot know or describe the nature of four adequately without presupposing the whole numerical system and therefore all these relations. I do not think we need deny that there are simple and unanalysable properties, on the contrary I cannot get away from the logical argument that the complex presupposes the simple. That there should be any synthetic *a priori* propositions connecting a simple property with other properties does seem incompatible, not indeed with its irreducibility by analysis, but with the notion that its full internal nature could be grasped apart from its relations to the other properties which are entailed by it, as Moore seemed to hold. May it not be that there are cases of properties which are indefinable in themselves and yet incapable of being understood apart from each other? Shape and size seem to be indefinable in the sense that no analysis could be produced which would make clear what they were to anybody who had not experienced them, or (if that were possible) had only experienced one and not the other, yet each entails the other and could not be understood without reference to it. Again, a term is something over and above its relations, otherwise the relations would not relate anything, but it does not follow that a term is always intelligible apart from its relations. Granted that a concept is simple and unanalysable, the correct point of view may be to look upon it not as for that reason intelligible in itself, but rather as being too much of an abstraction to stand by itself. This it may be just because it is simple.

Now I find it difficult to maintain that I can understand what goodness is quite apart from my knowledge of the nature of things which are good, or what moral obligation is quite apart from my knowledge of the kind of acts which are obligatory. This is not necessarily to deny that there is some indefinable flavour about the notion of goodness (or of obligation) itself which just cannot be reduced to any other properties or relations; but it does not seem to me that you can have a clear idea of this quality or relation without others, and not only without some other qualities or relations, but without some specific kinds of qualities or relations. It is unfortunate that Moore in his account of good took yellow as an illustration of another simple indefinable quality, because goodness and yellowness are such very different kinds of properties, but as a matter of fact even yellow is an example of what I have been saying. For it is not just a single quality but a class of shades, and nobody could grasp what "yellow" meant without being acquainted with several of these shades. Indeed I should go further and say that the notion of yellow was unintelligible apart from that of light (not in the sense in which "light" is used in physical science), and perhaps apart from that of colours other than yellow. However it is still less plausible to hold the view which Paton is attacking in regard to good. Goodness is rather of the nature of a categorial property, a very abstract universal, and, whatever may be the case with yellow, it is more than doubtful whether the nature of categorial properties can be grasped apart from the scheme or system of entities subject to the category. This is not the same as saying that we could not grasp the nature of goodness without knowing every good thing that has ever existed, but we must know some.

Now, if Paton is right, any coherent will, and (I suppose

in a different sense of "good") everything which is coherently willed, is good. The connection is not on his view contingent but necessary; and Moore would agree that anything which was good at all was so necessarily because of its other qualities. But if to be a case of coherent willing is necessarily to be good and vice versa, even though this may not give the *meaning* of good, it is difficult to see how the nature of the one concept could be grasped in complete abstraction from the nature of the other; and so, if Paton is right, we may both grant Moore's point that good cannot be defined in the sense of analysed, and yet insist with Paton that we cannot understand goodness except in relation to coherent willing. (Paton admits that his doctrine could be stated in terms of Moore's view.[4]) Goodness and a certain kind of coherence might be two different irreducible [5] and yet inseparable aspects of the same thing. Let us now consider whether they are inseparable.

It seems to me that there are different respects, not always distinguished, in which ethical principles might be said to be coherent:

(1) The coherence of ethical principles might be interpreted to mean simply formal logical consistency both internally and with each other. They undoubtedly must have this characteristic, otherwise they could not be true; and it cannot be disputed that consistency is a valuable test both for practical decisions and for a general theory of ethics. But unless we can show that there is a logical self-contradiction involved in denying the validity of ethics and can thus prove *a priori* some ethical propositions without already presupposing the truth of any other such propositions, we cannot make coherence in this sense the sole criterion and basis of

---

[4] Op. cit., p. 224.
[5] I do not mean to imply that coherence is unanalysable, only that it is not reducible to goodness, though perhaps necessarily connected with the latter. Indeed, as we shall see later, I do not hold that goodness is itself unanalysable.

ethics. Nobody has shown such a contradiction in the strict logical sense to be involved in refusing to assent to any particular ethical proposition, and it is certainly against any modern views of logic to suppose that it ever could be shown.

(2) There is, however, another kind of inconsistency, to which Kant makes reference, that is at least a frequent feature and a valuable criterion of wrong action. Kant does not claim that, for instance, to tell a particular lie is self-contradictory, but he holds that there would be a sort of self-contradiction in asserting or at least in trying to carry out the universal principle that everybody should tell lies whenever it suited them. For the principle would be self-defeating. What the liar wants is by no means that lying in general should be regarded as justified. He does not want other people to lie to him. Hitler showed no lack of ability to appreciate the badness of breaches of faith when he himself was the victim of one; for example, at the hands of Badoglio. What the liar wants is to make an exception in his own case. Now it may be said that this course of action is fundamentally inconsistent unless there are special circumstances relevant to the situation other than the fact that it is he himself (or somebody specially connected with him) who is concerned. If there is no relevant difference between two cases it is inconsistent to do A in the one and B in the other.

We may in fact distinguish two different kinds of inconsistency:

(a) There is the kind which consists in seeking A and then doing something which prevents or hinders my attainment of A; for example, going to somebody to come to an agreement with him and then wrecking or diminishing the prospects of agreement by an outburst of anger. We may admit that very much wrong action is inconsistent in this sense. It has even been contended that all wrong action is, on the ground that we desire ultimate satisfaction and that only right action will lead to this. But this inconsistency is certainly not the only circumstance which makes it wrong, otherwise an act would be right simply because it led to the agent's own satisfaction. It is more plausible to say that what makes an act right is that it tends ultimately to produce general satisfaction; but, apart from the hedonist and naturalist character of this view, which in my opinion lays it open to objection, it would not show that there was any inconsistency in wrong action. For it certainly cannot be maintained that everybody always desires the greatest satisfaction of people in general even when it conflicts with his own, and therefore to show that an action does not lead to this may be to show that it is wrong, but certainly is not to show that it is inconsistent or self-defeating.

But (b) there is a second kind of inconsistency, the kind which consists in doing or approving A on one occasion and B on another when there is no relevant difference between the set of circumstances on the two occasions to justify this distinction. This is the sort of inconsistency shown by the man who makes an unjustifiable profit himself, yet rails against profiteers in other articles which he wants to buy, or in its extreme form by a savage who, when asked whether he knew the difference between right and wrong, is reputed to have said: "Yes, if another man takes my wife, it is wrong; if I take another man's wife, it is right." There is a corresponding distinction in the realm of logic: a man may be inconsistent either in the sense of asserting or implying both p and not-p or in the sense of asserting in some cases a conclusion as following from evidence which in other cases he would never admit could lead to such a conclusion. In practical action inconsistency in the first sense is appropriately called imprudence or irrationality; in the second sense it is usually called unfairness.

It is this second kind of inconsistency to which Kant is

referring. When he insists that all lying is wrong because of its effects if universalized, he is not arguing that a particular lie is wrong because it will eventually harm the man who tells it. He is contending that it appertains to the nature of a rational being not to make exceptions in his own favour but only to adopt principles of action which he could consistently universalize. Why cannot we consistently universalize the principle that we should lie whenever it suits our interests? Because this principle would be self-defeating. The motive for lying is to further one's own interests, but, if everybody lied, our own interests would thereby be not furthered but defeated. Therefore, if we are to lie we must be inconsistent in the sense of claiming for ourselves what we could not allow to others. We must be inconsistent in the second sense because, if our policy were universally adopted, it would be inconsistent in the first. The fundamental injustice of the attitude of the man who profits by others obeying the law while he himself violates it is at any rate a reason against lying, even if it does not, as Kant thought, prove all lies without exception wrong. And it is very interesting to note that even a utilitarian like Hume finds himself forced to admit that there are cases where we ought to perform an action which by itself will do harm rather than good, on the ground that it is one of a class of acts which, taken together, do good rather than harm.*

A good instance of this is the case of paying taxes. Suppose a man to urge that he will miss the sum he has to pay much more than it would be missed by society. The absence of the few pounds which he has to pay will not, he may urge, make any perceptible difference whatever to the public funds, but it will make a very perceptible difference to himself, therefore to force him to pay it will do more harm than good; and it will be difficult to answer him if we consider the partic-

---

* *An Enquiry Concerning the Principles of Morals*, Appendix III.

ular act by itself. But the real answer surely is that he still ought to pay it, because this argument, if admitted at all, would apply to practically everybody, and it would therefore be unfair of him to benefit by other people's taxes while not paying his own share. (The unfairness would not arise if he had strong special grounds for exemption which did not apply to everybody.) It is a difficult question how far and under what circumstances we are to apply Kant's principle that we must not do what we could not will universalized, but it certainly supplies a valuable practical criterion in many cases where the utilitarian criterion as applied to the particular act would lead us wrong or be very uncertain.

This is not to say that it would be logically inconsistent for me, for instance, to lie in these cases. There is no logical inconsistency in doing what I believe to be wrong. But it would be logically inconsistent for me to maintain that I was doing right and yet that other people who lied under similar conditions were doing wrong. Nor is it to say that there are no possible exceptional cases in which I should be justified in doing what it would be wrong for most people under similar external circumstances to do. But in that case there would be an argument based on my psychology in favour of the action, which would not apply to people who had a different psychology. What would be inconsistent would be for me to try to justify my action by any argument which, if valid at all, would apply to everybody.

A somewhat similar distinction arises even in regard to purely prudential considerations: it is prudent for an undergraduate to work sufficiently to pass his examination, yet it may well be the case that in regard to any particular hour he can truly say that to spend this hour differently would give him more pleasure [7] and would not by itself jeopardise his chances

---

[7] The pleasure might even be qualitatively better; for example, its aesthetic value might be greater than the intrinsic intellectual value of an hour's study.

of passing, yet if he says that about every period of an hour and acts accordingly, he will certainly fail. Here, however, the question of neglect to perform the action being unfair to others by whose performance of the action we have benefited does not enter directly.

There are thus a good many acts which, as far as one can tell, do more harm than good, and yet are obligatory for the reason given, for example, paying taxes where the individual taxpayer misses the money much more than, if his particular contribution were not forthcoming, it would be missed by the community. I am not satisfied that this is the only reason why we ought not to tell lies or act unjustly—another reason, I hold, is that these activities are intrinsically evil—but at any rate it is one reason. We must note further that it can be applied only in cases where there is no ethically relevant difference between my case and the case of others. There might be special circumstances which made it right for me to be exempted from taxes, while other people paid them; all we can say is that, if this diversity of treatment is to be defended, I must be able to cite some special difference in my circumstances. The principle does not really therefore tell one much, but it does at any rate show that strict utilitarianism is not the true theory of ethics; and it is an important illustration of the part rational coherence plays in ethics. If an action is to be right, it must also be right for everybody in similar circumstances to act in the same way. It is not, however, the case that all duties can be deduced from this principle. To use the principle we must indeed know independently of it whether it would be right or wrong for everybody to act in this way. And the principle cannot by itself prove the intrinsic goodness or badness of anything.

(3) Logical "coherence," however, in the sense in which the term is used by holders of the "coherence" theory of truth does not mean mere consistency; it means that true proposi-

tions are supposed to form a system such that they are not divisible into logically independent groups but help to confirm one another's truth, and that none of them could be false while all the others (or perhaps even any of the others) remained true. I do not think it is worth while discussing whether coherence in this sense is the definition of "good" in at least Moore's sense of "definition," for I am not sure whether anybody has ever really meant to maintain this, and it is quite obviously false. But it may be maintained rather more plausibly that the criterion of the truth of an ethical judgement, whether we are thinking of one which expresses a general ethical theory or of a particular decision in practical life, is whether the judgement coheres with our other ethical judgements in a way which brings us nearer to such a system than we should be if we believed it false. This is at least one interpretation which might be given of the view. The coherence theory is indeed put forward as an ideal; it does not claim that we have already established such a coherent system either in ethics or in the realm of truth generally, but it does claim that the criterion of truth is the degree in which the propositions we assert to be true show a more or less feeble and inadequate approximation towards this coherence, and this would have to be understood as applying to true ethical judgements as well as to true judgements about anything else. Further, it is held that it is this coherence which makes them true. But this theory, in at least its unqualified form, seems to me again quite untenable, because it is not mere coherence with any sort of judgements, but at the most coherence with true judgements, which makes a judgement itself true.[8] The advocates of the coherence theory of truth have therefore commonly been forced to say that it is not mere coherence, but coherence plus comprehensiveness, or coherence with experience, which is, for us at least, the criterion; and a similar view, it seems,

---

[8] On this v. Ross in *Arist. Soc. Supp.*, Vol. X, pp. 61 ff.

would have to be taken in regard to ethical judgements. Suppose the judgement that A is good coheres with the judgements that B and C are good. This surely cannot be either what makes A good or a ground for affirming A to be good, unless we assume that B and C really are good? If they are not, coherence with the judgement that they are good is an argument against, rather than for, the truth of the judgement that A is good. And therefore, just as the coherence test will not work in regard to theoretical judgements unless we admit that there are truths based on sense experience with which the judgements have to cohere, so it will not work in ethics unless there are ethical truths apprehended intuitively with which other ethical judgements may be expected to cohere. The only way of replying to this would be if it could be maintained that there is one, and only one, coherent system of ethical propositions conceivable, but I do not know how this could be shown.

No doubt, granted some ethical propositions which we know by other means, coherence in the sense described above is a useful test. It is not only that, if we know some ethical propositions, any others inconsistent with these must be false; this will be true on any theory. It may be the case that some ethical judgements which we are inclined to make are not actually inconsistent with any others known to be true, but are of such a kind that they cannot be fitted into any systematic ethical theory. They cannot then be deduced from or rendered probable by any more general judgements which have their application also in other parts of ethics. If so, I should regard this as an argument against them as far as it goes. (The retributive theory of punishment I should take as an example.) The argument is not conclusive: after all, even if all true ethical judgements make up a completely coherent system, we cannot expect to be in a position to see the coherence in all cases, and we may be able to know by intuition the truth of certain ethical judgements which do not stand in any relation of entailment to others that we thus know. Further, if we do know the truth of an ethical judgement intuitively, any further test by coherence will be superfluous. But the value of the test is to be found in cases where we are not certain of the truth of an ethical judgement, but are inclined to believe it intuitively. Then, if it coheres positively in a system and is not merely logically compatible (non-contradictory) with other ethical judgements that we are inclined to believe, the different ethical judgements within the system will help to confirm each other. Thus intuition and coherence may help each other out as tests in cases where the intuition does not amount to knowledge. If there is no other justification whatever for thinking either p or q true, the fact that they cohere does not provide a ground; and if they are already known to be true, their coherence is not needed as a further ground for accepting them. But, if we are doubtful whether we can see them to be true or not, we may be thankful for coherence as an additional ground, which at least strengthens the probability of the various judgements which cohere with each other. For, if there is some probability both that p is true and that q is true, the fact that p and q are interrelated so that the one entails the other, or at least strengthens its probability, will increase the probability of both, since any grounds for the one will now support the other also.

The application of this test will be discussed later in the book, but I have said here sufficient to show that coherence in this sense is not the sole basis of goodness. That coherence or system is an important characteristic of the class of ethical propositions is in practice admitted by almost all writers on ethics. For they aim at systematizing their ethical data as far as they can, thus presupposing that the more they can do this the nearer they will be, *ceteris paribus*, to the truth; and a similar assumption is made in physical science. This is not to say that ethical propositions could necessarily ever fulfil the ideal of a completely coherent system; but it is clear that no philosopher believes that they cannot be brought into any sort of system, though opinions may differ very much as to the looseness or simplicity of the system. Nobody believes that every single ethical judgement is unique in such a way that we can never argue from one to another.

(4) But "coherence" as applied in ethics may mean something different from "coherence" in logic, because it may be held, as it is, for example, by Paton, that it is coherence in willing, or between different acts of will, which constitutes ethical goodness.[9] This relation of coherence between wills could obviously only be analogous to and not the same as the relation of coherence between propositions. Ethical goodness on that view consists in willing in such a way that one's different purposes will help, and not frustrate, each other, and that they bear the same relation of cooperation and mutual usefulness to the purposes of other men. Now it is clear that any fully adequate ideal includes a due development of all the different sides of life, so that they will not conflict with, but rather supplement and further each other. This ideal in its completeness is, short of immortality, quite unattainable, for the mere fact that time is limited, to speak of nothing else, makes it necessary to sacrifice one end worth pursuing to another. But it is one of the marks of a satisfactory as opposed to an unsatisfactory life that it is much nearer attaining this ideal. A bad life will either be much less integrated or much narrower than a good life. It will either be spoiled by a constant oscillation between conflicting ends, or be harnessed to the service of an end which impoverishes life by suppressing many of the real needs of our nature, for among these we must include the more altruistic side of man as well as the

---

[9] This is given by Paton as an account of what goodness is, not as its criterion (*The Good Will*, p. 368).

egoistic. Unfortunately an ethically good life may itself suffer from grave impoverishment owing to circumstances and may include the continuous struggle against and suppression of strong and normal desires involving a whole important side of a man's nature; but that this has to occur is admittedly an evil, though the person to whom it occurs may not deserve blame and may even deserve high praise for voluntarily sacrificing his potentialities for the sake of other men. If we look at the question from the point of view of humanity as a whole, we may think of ethical conduct as that conduct which is conducive to the cooperation of all in such a way that each man satisfies his own needs best by contributing to the common weal (though, since we are so far removed from this ideal good, the right thing to do may under present conditions very often be to deny one's own nature for the sake of others' good). But this again cannot be put forward as a definition of "good." That would constitute a vicious circle, for by "need" we must understand not any and every desire, but a desire which it is good should be fulfilled. If a man desires sadistic pleasures, it is not good that his desire should be attained, yet it is a real desire, and we only refuse to call it a real "need" because we judge that it is bad both for himself and others that the desire should be fulfilled. Have those who put forward this ideal then said anything more than that it is best that a man's actions should give him what is really good for himself and others what is really good for themselves? Yes, they have. For, besides its hortatory value in relation to certain political notions, what has been said calls attention to the important fact that the different goods (or, if this is preferred, the different *prima facie* duties) are so related to each other that on the whole the furtherance or performance of one helps the furtherance or performance of others and that their furtherance or performance in the case of one man helps their furtherance or performance in the case of other men. To say this is not a tautology; antecedently to a specific consideration of the nature of what is good it might conceivably, for anything we could know, have turned out to be the case that the good was like a store of food on a desert island, which could not be increased by cooperation and of which one individual could only have more at the expense of others, and it might have also turned out to be the case that there was no connection between the different kinds of good such that the attainment of one ever facilitated the attainment of others. That this is not the case is seen to follow, not from the abstract concept of good, but from the examination of the specific nature of goods.

We may think that this characteristic is bound up with the fundamental nature of good, but we obviously cannot say that what makes a thing good is always that it tends to contribute to the production of other goods. Still less could we make this a definition of "good." But it may be held that this is a characteristic which always necessarily accompanies goodness, though it could not have been discovered without considering not just the abstract nature of goodness, but the specific nature of the things which are good, and though it is not true without limitations except in the sense that, other things being equal, one good will *tend* to facilitate another. (That sometimes we have to sacrifice one good for the sake of another is obvious, and we can only say that it is not the essential tendency of good to demand this ultimate sacrifice.) In any case, to ask whether it contributes towards such a system in which all sides of life will be developed and harmonized and each man will work for the good of all and all for the good of each is no doubt a very useful question to ask about proposed actions and may serve as a criterion of their value. The world would have been a much better place if politicians had had this ideal more frequently present to their minds.

(5) But the coherence theory has also been interpreted as expressing the view that goodness consists in coherence with the realization of as many desires and the fulfilment of as many potentialities as possible. If this is taken as a definition of "good," the view is difficult to distinguish from the naturalist one that "good" means what satisfies desire, a doctrine that has been criticised in the previous chapter. But, if not a definition, is this at least an adequate description of a property essentially bound up with goodness? Now I think we must make a distinction here. It does seem that, if something is to be good, it must give satisfaction; but that it will satisfy in proportion to its goodness, even if it is known as it is, seems much more doubtful to me. It may be, as has often been suggested, that if we knew the good as it really was we should always desire it in proportion to its goodness; but how are we to know that we should? Conceivably, if Hitler had known at the time exactly what it felt like to be ill-treated, he would not have desired in any way to ill-treat the Jews; but I do not know how this could be proved. Still less do I see how we could establish the proposition that, if we knew fully what anything was like, our desire for it would correspond exactly to the degree of its goodness. It is an obvious fact that it does not always so correspond. Few people, if any, do not desire their own or their family's good more than the much greater good of a total stranger, even when they do not act on the desire. Few people would really rather have violent toothache than suffer a very slight deterioration of character, yet they would usually admit that the second was worse than the first. And in the absence of the complete knowledge referred to I do not know what empirical evidence there could possibly be for the view that, if we had it, this discrepancy would always be completely removed. But even supposing that it would be thus removed, this would still strike me as a quite contingent fact. I cannot see that it follows necessarily from the nature

of goodness: we may be built that way, and again we may not. As for the "fulfilment of potentialities," I cannot see that this is good at all unless we first know that the potentialities are good potentialities. We cannot even say that right action or a good life fulfils more potentialities than does the reverse, since for each potentiality for good there must be at least one potentiality for evil (in fact many, since where you can do what is right in one way you can always deviate from it in many). On the other hand, it is important to insist that the good does satisfy, and that on the whole (though with many exceptions in human life) the greater good will ultimately give the fuller satisfaction.

(6) "Coherence" may be used loosely to mean any sort of harmony. It is certainly a mark of right action and good living on the whole that it conduces to harmony both within the self and between different persons; but it is not so clear that harmony is the sole criterion of goodness or the sole characteristic which makes anything good. For (a) an increase in goodness may result in a loss of harmony. A man who consistently cheats without compunction is in a more harmonious state of mind than he would be if he had improved sufficiently to hesitate, upbraid himself, and struggle against the temptation, but not sufficiently in most cases to overcome it; and a good man will be less in harmony with a bad society, such as Nazi Germany, than a bad man would. (b) One of the greatest goods is the heroic struggle against difficulties, which can hardly be described as a case of harmony. (c) Harmony cannot be the only good, if once it is admitted that a harmony involving richer content is preferable to the harmony of a very unintelligent and limited mind with few moral ideas. A fortiori, "good" cannot be defined as harmony. This would also be open to the objections to a naturalist definition, unless ethical content was already smuggled into the notion of harmony, thus involving a vicious circle in the definition; and

it would involve a confusion between the notion of goodness and the notion of what is good. Harmony is good, but it is not goodness, nor is it the only characteristic which makes what possesses it good.

The present discussion should have made it clear that the same applies to all the different interpretations of "coherence" discussed. None of them can be regarded as giving either the analysis or the sole ground of goodness, but they do all bring out important features of the good life. Important features of ethical action are that it is not self-defeating, that it can be universalized, that it can be fitted into a coherent plan of life, that it finds one's own good in serving that of others, that it is internally harmonious and subserves harmonious relations with other men. But these properties are at the most necessarily connected, and not identical, with the quality of good.

Paton does not use "definition" either in Moore's sense or in the sense merely of exclusive description, but still in some sense of "definition" which admits necessary connection and even substantial, though not absolute, identity between *definiendum* and *definiens*. In this sense he defines "good" as "aimed at by a rational will," or, as applied to human beings, that will itself. Now to me a "rational will" means "a will which wills what it ought," but this would still be a definition of "good" in ethical terms, and one which is like the definition that I shall give later. Only this of course is not all that Paton meant by the phrase. On the other hand he did not mean merely either a will which takes the steps most adapted to securing its own satisfaction or a logically coherent will. Coherence in action is for him analogous to coherence in thought but not identical with it. His definition then seems to amount to asserting that good is a quality of the will or (in a different sense) of objects of the will, and that it is analogous to logical coherence in a very important way. This statement seems somewhat jejune, but it acquires concrete filling and interest by the admirable way in which the analogy is brought out in the actual content of the book. That, in one sense of the word, "good" is a quality which can only apply to the will and in another only to objects of the will I admit, and I have also pointed out its connection with coherence. But I should prefer not to call this a definition of "good" as attribute of the will, but rather an account of it which brings out its analogy to logical coherence. Possibly he may have even shown that goodness is, on one side of its nature, a species of coherence, logical coherence being another species. By saying "one side of its nature" I wish to exclude the view that goodness of will is just a species of coherence in the sense in which yellow is just a species of colour and to avoid committing myself to the denial of the possibility that it might be equally appropriately made also a species of some other genus. I should certainly not wish to say that "good" in any ordinary sense just meant "coherence in willing."

Let us turn to other non-naturalist definitions of "good."

Prof. Broad once suggested in his lectures a new type of analysis of "good," not indeed as his own theory, but as a view worth discussion. He suggested that "A is good" might mean "there is one and only one characteristic or set of characteristics whose presence in any object that I contemplate is necessary to cause an emotion of approval in me, and A has that characteristic." What the characteristic is in itself we do not know, but only its effects on our emotions. This view does not therefore make "good" equivalent to the property of causing an emotion, but to the unknown characteristic which causes the emotion. Since this characteristic may for anything we can tell be either naturalist or non-naturalist, it is impossible to apply either term to this theory, the "descriptive theory," as Broad called it, of "good." As he pointed out, it might be the case that a character which was itself non-naturalist could only be conceived by us as the character which was related to our experience in a certain way, and in that case it would without being itself given in experience answer to a description in which all the terms were naturalist. In that case "good" would be indefinable, by us at least, in Moore's sense, since we could not reduce it to anything else to which it was exactly equivalent, but definable in the sense that we could give an exclusive, though not exhaustive, description of it. The description would not give the nature of goodness, but it would provide relations by which to identify it. And the only evidence for something being good would still consist of empirical facts. This is not a view which Broad himself holds, but it is a conceivable alternative that is worth a short discussion at any rate.

Broad works the theory out in terms of the relation of goodness to the emotions of the speaker, but it might also be worked out in relation to the emotions of most people. Or again it might be worked out in terms not of the emotion of approval but of desire, and it might be said that goodness was that characteristic whose presence in anything, x, is necessary to enable x to satisfy human desires. In fact for every naturalist theory (not every subjectivist theory) of "good" we might have a "descriptive" theory of "good." And a similar treatment might be applied to any naturalist definition of "right"— for example as that characteristic whose presence in any action is necessary if that action is to be commended by society— though of course some of these descriptive theories would be less plausible than others.

At any rate the suggested theory seems to me to be open in all cases to serious objections. In the first place, we sometimes know, it would seem indeed with absolute, but at the very least with almost complete, certainty, that something is good or bad. But we could never know or even have a right to be confident of this if the descriptive theory were true. As Broad admitted: "If the descriptive theory is correct, then every judgement of the form 'x is good' that I have ever made has been false unless there is one and only one characteristic or set of characteristics whose presence in any object that I can contemplate is necessary to make me contemplate it with approval." Now if, as admitted, we have no idea what the characteristic in question is like, I do not see how we could ever be justified in being very confident, let alone know, that the same characteristic or set of characteristics was present in everything of which we felt approval and was a necessary condition of our having the feeling. The feeling might well be due to different characteristics on different occasions, and no one of these might be a necessary condition of its occurrence; or it might be the case that the only characteristic which was a necessary condition of our feeling of approval was present also in things of which we had no tendency to feel approval and which were not good.

Could the theory be amended to meet this objection? I doubt it. It would not do to define "good" as *any* characteristic of the several whose presence may be necessary if something is to arouse the emotion of approval, because if there were several conditions and one or more were missing the thing in question might well be the reverse of good. For instance, it is plausibly held that being a conscious state of some mind is a characteristic necessarily present in anything which is intrinsically good or gives rise to approval, but it is certainly also a characteristic of many things which are bad or indifferent. Nor would it do to define "good" as a characteristic which constitutes a sufficient condition for exciting the emotion of approval. For the sufficient condition would in any case include a great complexity of circumstances many of which could not possibly be called good-in-themselves, including, for example, certain physical conditions in the observer without which he could not feel the emotion. Nor again could we define "good" as any characteristic which *tends* to excite an emotion of approval, for the characteristic of being a painful experience of a hated person does, yet that does not prove the characteristic to be good. It may be objected that the approval in this case is not the moral emotion of approval, but if A really hates B there is at least a *tendency* in A to feel the emotion of moral approval of the sufferings of B under the belief or "rationalization" that they are a just punishment for his sins. (No doubt it is not "moral" in the sense of right, but the descriptive theory was not meant to define "good" as that towards which it was right to feel an emotion of approval—otherwise it would come much closer to the theory I propose in a later chapter to defend—and there is no psychological distinction between an emotion of approval felt on a right occasion and one felt on a wrong one.) Moreover practically all men have a tendency to feel more disapproval at wrong acts directed against their friends than at similar acts directed against strangers, yet it does not follow that the former are therefore worse acts. If, on the other hand, we merely say that "A is good" means "A has some qualities or other which make most men approve it," we have said hardly anything more than if we had just said that it means "most men approve it." If most men approve it, it must have some qualities or other which make most men approve it.

In any case goodness is surely a property the presence of which we know directly sometimes, at least in our own experiences, and not one which we hypothetically suppose to account for a similarity in our emotions. It seems to me quite impossible to make the question whether something is good turn on whether there is some unknown characteristic which is a necessary causal condition of our approval. It is logically conceivable that physiologists might sometime discover that the production of a certain physical modification of the brain was a condition which was fulfilled in all cases when something caused the emotion of approval in a person and on no other occasions, but would that justify them in identifying the property of goodness with this modification or the capacity of producing it? This illustration shows it to be at least logically possible that a characteristic other than goodness may be a necessary condition of approval, therefore being good cannot be identical with being a necessary condition of approval. We are extremely interested for itself in whether things are good; we are not interested for itself in the question whether there is one and the same unknown property present in all of them.

Nor does the theory seem to escape at least most of the objections which I have directed against naturalism. It is admitted that, on the descriptive theory, the only evidence for the truth of an ethical judgement lies in empirical facts about people's emotions. Now, as Broad himself very rightly objected in criticizing Hume, "the logical consequence of his theory . . . is that the way to settle ethical disputes is to collect statistics of how people in fact do feel. And to me this kind of answer seems utterly irrelevant to this kind of question. If I am right in this, Hume's theory must be false." [10] But surely the same objection might now be applied to the descriptive theory? And I do not see how we can judge that this notion of an unknown condition behind our emotions of approval carries with it the notion of obligation any more than the mere fact that we have a certain feeling could. Since we do not on that view know what the quality goodness is, we cannot say that the contemplation of it either directly excites our approval or puts us under an obligation, for we cannot contemplate goodness at all.

Another definition of "good," which might be regarded either as naturalist or as logical or even as metaphysical, is in terms of the notion of a good (typical or characteristic) speci-

---

[10] *Five Types of Ethical Theory*, p. 115.

men of a class. (It should be noted that this attempt at definition, unlike any of the others discussed, takes as the primary sense of "good" that in which it is applied to an individual as a whole, not to a single experience.) No doubt if "typical" means "like most other members of its class," such a view would not be worth the least consideration. An advocate of the definition would rather regard goodness as consisting in fulfilling the characteristic function of the species not with average but with specially great effectiveness. And he would distinguish what functions of the species are characteristic by asking what it is that members of the species can do which members of other species cannot do at all or cannot do so efficiently. The definition may be viewed either as logical because it depends on the logical relation between member and class, or as naturalist because it defines the ethical wholly in non-ethical terms that might occur in other sciences. It may even be viewed as metaphysical if its upholder goes on to say that, just as goodness relative to one's species consists in the fulfilment of the tendency characteristic of that species, so goodness in an absolute sense consists in what makes for the fulfilment of the tendency characteristic of reality as a whole. In that way it can be connected either with evolutionary or with theological ethics. For the sciences which study the evolutionary process may be regarded as disclosing empirically the leading tendencies in the real world; and theology is bound up with the conviction that the fundamental nature of reality is in accord with the highest ethical ideals that can be conceived, so that to act well is to act in a way which is in harmony with the ultimate purpose of the universe and the ultimate nature of things.

In criticism of any such definition we may urge that it would not be self-contradictory to say that something was good (in almost all senses of the word) and yet to deny that it was a typical specimen of its class. The sense in which we can speak of a "good burglar" is clearly a special and paradoxical sense of "good." We can also be certain that something is good and yet extremely doubtful whether it is typical of its class. To fulfil the function of one's class efficiently is not to be good, unless it is good that this particular function should be fulfilled, a question which could only be decided by examining it on its own merits. It seems to me that the kind of view under discussion would turn out to be exposed either to the objections which I have already brought against naturalist theories, or to the objections which I shall bring directly against theological theories, or to both together. The notion of doing efficiently what one's class normally does is not one from which obligation can be derived. Why *ought* I to act like typical members of my class? If it is said that goodness consists in the fulfilment of the function which I was designed to fulfil, the reply may be made that this cannot carry with it an obligation unless we assume that the designer is good, and in order to be entitled to maintain this we must already presuppose independent ethical ideas. We cannot arrive at an ethical conception of God without already having an idea of what goodness is. Consideration of this brings one to theological views of ethics.

A theological definition of ethical terms is the commonest and most intelligible type of metaphysical definition, and the natural form it would assume would be that "A ought to be done" is to be analysed as "A is commanded by God." At first sight it seems as if such a theory were refuted at once by the mere fact that an atheist or agnostic can judge that something ought to be done; but it might be said that what even the atheist really has in his mind when he thinks of moral obligation is some confused idea of a command, and that a command implies a commander and an ethically valid command a perfectly good commander on whose mind the whole moral law depends. In that case the atheist would be inconsistent in denying or even doubting the existence of God and yet insisting on the validity of the moral law, which he could justify only by assuming what he doubted or denied. But there is an important distinction to be made. I do not intend to discuss here whether such an argument, or any argument based on ethics, for the existence of God is valid; but I must insist that to say that ethical concepts properly thought out can provide an argument for or even logically entail the existence of God would not be the same as to say that a reference to God is included in their definition. To take an analogous case, anybody who believes in the argument from design argues to the existence of God from certain features of animal bodies, but it would never occur to him to say that our concepts of these purely biological features must therefore be analysed in such a way as already to include the notion of God. His biology would still be like anyone else's and would not be based on concepts referring to God. This would still be true even if he accepted the cosmological proof and so held that the existence of this world entailed and did not merely provide evidence for the existence of God. If God exists he is the *ratio essendi* of the beings from whom we argue to God, but he is not for us their *ratio cognoscendi* since we cannot deduce their nature from his. And even if it be the case that the whole moral law depends on God, this is not to say that in order to reach moral conceptions we have first to form a conception of God. A theist holds that trees or stones could not exist without God; but he will not therefore insist that all our commonsense propositions about trees and stones have to be analysed in such a way as to include the notion of God.

To a theological definition of the fundamental ethical concepts there seem to me to be fatal objections, though these objections must not be taken as excluding the possibility that we might be able to argue from ethical premises to the existence of God, as was indeed held by Kant, the strongest defender of the autonomy of ethics from other studies including theology. In the first place, if "obligatory" just means "commanded by God," God cannot command an act because it is right, and there is no reason whatever for his commands, which therefore become purely arbitrary. It would follow that God might just as rationally will that our whole duty should consist in cheating, torturing, and killing people to the best of our ability, and that then it would be our duty to act in that fashion. I am assuming that "good" is defined in the same kind of way as "obligatory." Otherwise it might be held that God commanded acts because they produced good, but in that case we should not have given a theological definition of all the fundamental ethical concepts, and we should be either falling back on an indefinable "good" or adopting one of the definitions of it that I have already criticised.

Secondly, why obey God's commands? Because I ought to do so? Since "I ought to do A" is held to mean "God commands me to do A," this can only mean that I am commanded by God to obey God's commands, which supplies no further reason. Because I love God? But this involves the assumptions that I ought to obey the commands of God if I love him, and that I ought to love God. So it again presupposes ethical propositions which cannot without a vicious circle be validated by referring once more to God's commands. Because God is good? This could on the view under discussion only mean that God carries out his own commands. Because God will punish me if I do not obey? This might be a very good reason from the prudential point of view, but these considerations of self-interest cannot be an adequate basis for ethics. Even if there is some affinity between command and obligation, a mere command, however powerful the being who issues it, cannot of itself create obligation. Without a prior conception of God being good or his commands being right God would have no more claim on our obedience than Hitler except that he would have more power than even Hitler ever had to make things uncomfortable for those who disobeyed him. It is only because the notion of God (for Christians at least, not to mention other religions) already includes the notion of perfect goodness that we are inclined to think it self-evident that we ought to obey God. And even if it were self-evident, without presupposing this, that we ought to obey God's commands, the proposed analysis of "ought" still could not be accepted. It is plain that the sentence "We ought to obey God's commands" does not just mean "We are commanded by God to obey his commands." But in any case it is obvious that doing what one ought could not be equated with obeying the commands of any sort of God but only with obeying those of a *good* God.

It should be noted that there is a certain similarity between the theological view I have criticised and naturalism. For, as we could find no necessary relation between goodness and obligation on the one hand and the alleged naturalist definitions on the other, so we can find no necessary relation between being commanded by God and being obligatory, unless we already assume the goodness of God, thus exposing ourselves to a vicious circle, for we should in that case have both defined God in terms of goodness and goodness in terms of God. Just as it was a fatal objection to the naturalist definitions of "good" that they did not provide any ground for obligation or reason for doing any one thing rather than any other, so the theological definition is open to the objection that a command cannot in itself be a moral reason for action. Like naturalist definitions the theological definition would destroy what Kant calls the autonomy of ethics by refusing to recognise the uniqueness of its fundamental concepts and trying to make it a mere branch of another study, in this case not a natural science but theology. Both types of view overlook the gulf between the "ought" and the "is" so far as to think that you can reduce propositions about the former to mere statements as to what actually is the case. The theological view is more ethical than the naturalist only in so far as it covertly reintroduces the concept of obligation which it had verbally tried to explain away by equating it with a mere command. Except in so far as it smuggles the concept in again it makes the fulfilment of duty consist just in obeying the stronger, for if you once exclude the specifically ethical element from the concept of the deity God has no claim on us except that of mere power. Similar objections, besides others, can, I think, be turned against any one who, whether or not he defines ethical concepts in theological terms, claims that ethics is somehow to be derived from theology. But they do not necessarily hold against the view that you can derive theological conclusions, partly or wholly, from ethical premises.

Some thinkers have tried to provide a metaphysical definition of "good" in terms not of God but of our "real self." We may even accuse Kant of having sometimes come at least perilously near to this, inconsistent as it is with his main attitude to ethics. Theories of the real self are particularly difficult to discuss owing to their obscurity, which is partly no doubt the fault of their authors, but partly also due to the real difficulty of the subject. In one form the theory of the "real self" is a species of naturalism, amounting to the assertion that "good" means what would satisfy us ultimately or would satisfy us if we knew its true nature. In another form it is a type of theological ethics, God being regarded as immanent instead of transcendent, and the notion that something is good because it or the striving for it is commanded being superseded by the notion that it is good because it satisfies our "true" nature which is somehow bound up with that of all other selves. But that it will satisfy me is no reason for seeking anything unless I assume that my satisfaction is good, and the addition of the word "true" does not alter this, unless "true" is being used to mean "good," in which case the definition is obviously useless. The theory is, further, open to the objection that it would lead to an egoistic view of ethics unless *myself* is used in such a wide sense as to include all other selves, in which case the meaning of the term and therefore the point of the definition is destroyed. But I think upholders of such theories had usually no intention of defining "good" in Moore's sense of "definition." They may or may not have succeeded in discovering important truths about goodness, good things, and the nature of the real, but they certainly did not succeed in showing and probably did not in most cases intend to show that ethical concepts are reducible to non-ethical.

The main upshot of all the discussion in this book so far is the defence of the view that we must recognise that ethics is a branch of study of its own which cannot be reduced to or derived from any other. Good, right, obligation are not at all like non-ethical concepts and cannot be reduced to them. This is not necessarily to deny that they are intimately related to some non-ethical concepts, but it is to assert that they cannot just be identified with any combination of such concepts. It is now for us to go on to the more positive task of considering the relations between the different non-natural concepts of ethics itself.

CHAPTER IV

Different Meanings of "Good" and "Ought"

We shall pass in due course to another definition of "good" which is not open to the same objections as the definitions which I have discussed, but since "good" and "ought" are very ambiguous words it will be wise first to distinguish various senses in which they are used, and the present chapter will be devoted to this essential preliminary.

In the first place I must remind the reader (1) that, whether a naturalist view of ethics be right or not, it is certainly true that "good" is sometimes used in a purely naturalist, psychological sense to mean "pleasant." When I say "This pudding is good" I do not think I mean anything more than that I like it or find it pleasant, with the possible implication that most other people would do so too.

Similarly, (2), when I talk of somebody's good, I may only mean what will satisfy his desires.[1]

But I may also mean what is "really to his good," as when I say that it is not to a man's good to have everything that he wants, and the two meanings shade into each other so that it is often difficult to tell which is intended. This is because it is usually assumed that to have one's desires satisfied is for one's real good, provided they are not positively immoral desires. To say that something is for a man's good is to say that it will directly or indirectly result in a part of his life being better in some way (not necessarily hedonistically) than would

---

[1] V. Carritt, *An Ambiguity of the Word "Good."*

112

otherwise be the case without a counterbalancing loss somewhere else in his life. If "better" is being used naturalistically, this will probably mean only that his desires will be more fully satisfied; but the word may also be used differently, and then it will fall under one of the other senses of "good" to be enumerated later.

It is clear also that "good" is very often, perhaps most often, used in an instrumental sense to signify "good as a means," which sense has, almost from time immemorial, been distinguished from "good-in-itself." But the term "instrumentally good" or "good as a means" is itself ambiguous. It may mean —and this gives another naturalist sense of "good"—(3) capable of doing a particular kind of thing efficiently, whether that thing be itself good, bad, or indifferent. A knife might still be a "good knife" even if it were never used for anything but the most atrocious murders.

(4) *"Good as a means"* may also mean "productive of something intrinsically good." In this sense we speak of pure water as good and impure water as bad. Pure water, while more efficient as a means of maintaining health than impure water, is far less efficient as a means of producing typhoid fever; but we look on typhoid fever as evil or necessarily accompanied by intrinsic evils, while we look on health, which is maintained by pure water, as intrinsically good, or necessarily or probably accompanied by what is intrinsically good, and therefore we speak of pure water as good and impure water as bad. The distinction between (3) and (4) is still clearer in the case of "bad." We may call somebody or something bad just because it is inefficient, or we may call it bad because it is all too efficient in producing intrinsically bad effects. For example, diseases and hurricanes are called in this sense bad, though not themselves intrinsically bad.

(5) "Good" may mean not "efficient in producing effects" but rather "efficiently produced." I think this is the most usual

meaning of a "good book," a "good stroke at cricket," etc.

(6) It is obvious, however, that these senses (at least 4 and 5) presuppose a further, more primary sense of "good." This sense is commonly expressed by the terms "intrinsically good," "good-in-itself," "good as an end." There would be no point in being efficient if we could not thereby produce something that was good as an end and not only as a means.

But there is a point I wish to mention here. By calling a thing "intrinsically good" or "good-in-itself" I do not mean to commit myself to the view that it would necessarily be good in all contexts or could still be good if everything else in the universe were different. "Good-in-itself" has been used in this sense; but it need not imply this, as far as I can see. What I mean by "good-in-itself" is simply "good itself," in opposition to good as a means; that is, I mean that the thing called good really has the characteristic goodness in its primary sense, and is not merely called good because it produces something else which has the quality in question. As far as I can see, something might really have the characteristic goodness in some contexts and yet not have it in others, or have it only in a lower degree, as a poker is really hot when placed near the fire and not hot or not so hot when placed elsewhere.

Again, there is nothing to exclude a thing being both good in itself and good as a means in any ordinary sense of the latter term. The things that are intrinsically best themselves are also most likely to produce intrinsically good effects.

(7) Moore makes a distinction between "ultimately" and "intrinsically good." [2] Anything is intrinsically good, provided it contains elements which are good for their own sake, even if it also contains elements which are quite indifferent, provided only the other elements do not actually counteract the value of the good part. Such a thing would still be good

---

[2] *Ethics*, pp. 73-5.

even if it existed alone, he says, and he therefore calls it intrinsically good; but he will call something ultimately good only if it has no parts which are not themselves intrinsically good, so this gives a seventh sense of "good," ultimately good. In the sixth sense a successful life or a long holiday might be described as good, but it could hardly be called good in the seventh sense because the best holiday and, still more, the best life will contain stretches which are indifferent in respect of value, or at any rate stretches which are unpleasant rather than pleasant and in which there are no other values realised adequate to counteract this unpleasantness.

It is not clear whether it is the sixth or the seventh sense of "good" which should in preference be regarded as indefinable. In the passage mentioned Moore defines the seventh in terms of the sixth sense—what is "ultimately good" is something intrinsically good which either has no parts or has parts which are all intrinsically good—so presumably he regarded the sixth sense as primary. It might be argued that it would be better to take the reverse course on the ground that it is the ultimately good parts belonging to it which make anything intrinsically good, but this does not agree with Moore's principle of organic unities according to which something in itself indifferent or even bad might increase the intrinsic goodness of the whole to which it belonged. Usually no distinction has been made between these two senses, but I think the term "intrinsically good" has generally been used to express the seventh rather than the sixth sense of good.

"Good" is also often used to mean "either instrumentally or intrinsically or ultimately good," where the speaker believes something is good in one of these senses but has not thought it necessary to ask which (as indeed it often is not for purposes of practice). But we should swell our list of meanings so far as to exhaust the patience of the reader if we assigned a separate heading for each such unprecise usage of "good."

(8) "Good" in sense (6) or sense (7) is not properly applied to characteristics. When "good" is applied to a characteristic of something it signifies not that the characteristic is intrinsically good itself, but that things which have the characteristic are in so far intrinsically good. Thus we get an eighth sense of "good," in which "good" means good-making, to use Broad's terminology. In this sense "good" is applied to qualities to signify that the quality in question makes the things which have it good in sense 6 or sense 7. For example, the statement that pleasure is good means that the quality of pleasantness makes what has it good.

(9) "Good" often means morally good. Obviously moral goodness is not the only kind of intrinsic goodness, and it may possibly be denied that it is a case of intrinsic goodness at all, yet the people who deny this would still use of it the term "good." But this must be a matter for further discussion. In the sense of "morally good," the term is applied both to men and to actions, but it can hardly be applied to both in the same sense, so we now get both a ninth sense, "good" means "morally good" as applied to actions, and a tenth, "good" means "morally good" as applied to persons. No doubt "good" as applied to persons may also mean merely "efficient" (sense 3), for example, when we speak of a man as a good cricketer or a good philosopher, but it obviously sometimes stands for a more specifically moral quality.

Laird also introduces the concept of "dominant good" as of fundamental importance, meaning by this a good "which, irradiating its surroundings, dignifies whatever it touches"; [3] but I am not sure that this is not better regarded as a description of a particular species of good thing than as a different sense of "good." Moore also points out that "good" is sometimes used to mean "adding to the value of many intrinsically good wholes." [4]

---

[3] *A Study in Moral Theory*, p. 46.
[4] *Ethics*, p. 250.

Another sense of "good" which is sometimes admitted is "typical of its species," [5] but I think this is reducible to some of the other senses mentioned above. A thing is most commonly called a good specimen of its class because it is more efficient than the average member of the class in fulfilling certain ends, namely, those characteristic of the class or those for which that class of thing was made. It may also be called "a good specimen of the class" because it is a useful sample for the purposes of research. And, finally, it may be called a good specimen because it provides a certain aesthetic satisfaction, that is, something good in senses 6 and 7, for aesthetic satisfactions should be regarded as intrinsically valuable and not valuable merely in a naturalist sense.

Corresponding to the ten senses of "good" there are ten senses of "bad." "Bad" may mean (1) unpleasant; (2) contrary to what we desire; (3) inefficient in fulfilling certain purposes, whether these are themselves good, bad or indifferent; (4) productive of something intrinsically evil; (5) inefficiently made; (6) intrinsically bad, in Moore's sense as applied to particulars; (7) ultimately bad as applied to particulars; (8) as applied to qualities, such as to make what has it bad in the sixth or seventh sense; (9) morally bad as applied to actions; (10) morally bad as applied to persons. "Evil" is synonymous with "bad," except that it is not customarily used unless the degree of badness is very serious, and it could not, I think, correctly be applied to what was considered bad only in senses 1,2,3, or 5, except as a piece of "slang." It has therefore, unlike "bad," no purely naturalist sense at all.

The terms "good" and "bad" are thus extremely ambiguous, and in ethical discussion it is therefore most important to be clear in which sense we are using them. It is obvious, however, that sense 6 or sense 7 is fundamental and is of very special importance for philosophers. We have now come to the con-

---

[5] For the attempt to make this the main definition of good v. above, pp. 104-6.

clusion that in these senses at any rate "good" cannot be natu-ralistically defined. Of the other senses some are definable in terms of (6) or (7), others may be naturalistically defined. Senses 9 and 10 at least seem definable in terms of another non-naturalist ethical concept, ought. I shall now turn to the terms "ought," "right," "duty." It is obvious that these have a close relation to each other and that their chief application is to actions. They are not such ambiguous words as "good"; but there are at least three different usages of them in ethics which it is very important for the philosopher to distinguish. I shall explain the three different usages in the case of "ought." [*]

1. "The action we ought to do" may mean that action which is really preferable, taking everything into account. This would be the action which an omniscient and perfectly wise being would advise us to perform; but it is impossible for us to take everything into account, and it may even be doubted whether any action that ought to be done in this sense has ever in the whole of history been performed by a human being. For, whatever benefits I may produce by a certain expenditure of time or money, it seems in the highest degree likely that a being who knew all the circumstances and foresaw all the consequences could suggest some expenditure still more beneficial. For example, such a being would know the cure for cancer and would know how to prove to the medical profession that it was a cure. Now obviously to in-form medical experts of the right cure and persuade them to adopt it, if I could do this, would be a more beneficial action than any which I am likely to perform during my life in the normal course and would be an action that ought to be carried out immediately to save life and suffering, so that whatever I

---

[*] In *Philosophy*, Vol. XXI, No. 79, pp. 110–11, Professor Broad distin-guishes three senses of "right." The first and third respectively correspond to my first and second, but Broad's second ("formally right") does not cor-respond to my third.

do now such a being could advise me of something more beneficial to do instead; that is, take steps to bring about the adoption of the method of cure. It may be retorted that at any
rate I know that I ought to pay my debts and this could not
be altered even by the information of an omniscient being,
but "pays a debt" is an incomplete description of an act. I am
under an obligation to pay my debts; but I am not under an
obligation to pay them this very moment, especially where
there is some other pressing obligation, and hardly anybody
would expect me to keep an appointment if, as in this case, the
lives of many people depended on my missing it. Besides, even
in the case of paying debts, such a being could probably suggest something in my manner of doing it which would have
better effects than my present manner of doing it,[7] and could
certainly suggest some mental state in repaying the debt
preferable to the one actually experienced by me. It is highly
doubtful whether the mental state of any human being is ever
completely and absolutely ideal even for a moment. It seems
to me therefore objectionable to take the present as the main
sense of "ought," "right" or "duty," as is done, for example,
by Moore in his *Ethics*,[8] at least when we are applying "ought"
to actions regarded as a whole. It is surely desirable to use the
word in a sense in which we can be confident that there are
actions to which it applies. It is unsatisfactory to choose a
meaning for the word which makes it necessary to say that
probably no human being in the whole course of history has
ever acted as he ought. On the other hand, there is plenty of
scope for this sense of "ought" when not applied to actions
regarded as a whole. We can use it of what have been called
prima faci? duties, and say that in the absence of a conflicting

---

[7] I am not assuming that the consequences are the only factor in determining whether one action is preferable to another, but only that they are at least
highly relevant to this question.

[8] P. 190 ff.

obligation we ought always to keep a promise in this sense of "ought." We can also say in this sense that we ought to prefer certain ends to certain others, for example that we ought to value justice rather than money, and that certain emotional attitudes are fitting or unfitting towards certain kinds of objects, for example, we ought to dislike cruelty, we ought to love good parents. For here the complications about consequences do not arise, it being rather a question of the intrinsic value of something, so that if we had made any mistake in such judgements it would be a mistake of value and not of fact. We are rightly so confident of the truth of many such judgements that we use the term "know" rather than "believe," and the objection that probably no human being has ever done as he ought is certainly not applicable here. I am convinced that I ought to dislike the unnecessary infliction of pain, and not only that relatively to the available evidence I ought to do so; and this is not contradicted by the fact that it might under certain circumstances be the least undesirable course for me to choose to do something which gave much pain, and even which by an unfortunate concatenation of circumstances encouraged people to take pleasure in the pain; for example, if I take steps to secure the punishment of a criminal.

2. "Ought," both in philosophy and in ordinary discussion, is also used in a sense in which not to do what one ought, or to do what one ought not to do, is always morally blameworthy. To say that I ought to do A in this sense is indeed not the same as saying that I believe I ought to do A, for the proposition that I ought to do what I believe I ought to do is synthetic, but it is, I think, synthetic *a priori*. This sense of the word is extremely important, but it obviously presupposes another sense. That is made clear by considering the principle that we always ought to do what we believe we ought. We may believe, for example, that the soldiers who fight

against us in a war are acting wrongly in fighting, yet every reasonable person will admit that, as long as they really think they ought to fight, they ought "to obey their consciences" and fight. In general, it is clear that a person may make a mistake and decide that he ought to do A, though A is really wrong. In that case he clearly ought to do A, therefore he ought to do what is wrong, that is, what he ought not to do. Self-contradiction can only be avoided if we suppose that "ought" is being used in two different senses here. Again, if there is no sense of "ought" in which it is false to say that we always ought to do what we think we ought, we could discover what we ought to do by mere introspection without considering anything else whatever. These paradoxes can only be met by recognising another sense of "ought" besides the sense in which not to do what one "ought" is always morally blameworthy, and we have seen that the first sense is not adequate. So a third sense is required.

3. "The action which I ought to perform" may mean the action which it is, humanly speaking, preferable to choose, though it may not in fact necessarily turn out best. It seems to me that this is the sense in which the term "ought" is most commonly employed. We should not usually say that a man had not done what he ought just because some unforeseeable accident had changed the consequences from good to bad. It would be a very unusual use of language to say that I had done something which I ought not to have done because a man whom I had invited to tea was run over and killed on his way to my house; and if I saw somebody about to drink a glass of prussic acid and refrained from warning him, it would hardly be said that I had done what I ought because it was a new variety of prussic acid just discovered which was harmless or the man had such an abnormal physiology that he could drink prussic acid with impunity, if I had no knowledge of this circumstance but believed that the drink would bring

about his death. Likewise no one would say that I had acted wrongly or had not done my duty in the first case, or that I had acted rightly or had done my duty in the second. We rarely employ these terms in our first sense, but we do employ them in our third sense very frequently. A good example of the difficulties which arise from not making the distinction between the first sense and the third sense is provided by Professor Prichard in his paper on *Duty and Ignorance of Fact*.

We may explain the third sense further by saying that in this sense we ought to perform an act if in the light of the available evidence it seems the preferable act to choose. By "available evidence" I mean evidence which the agent either possesses already or could obtain without more trouble than is practicable or worth while, everything considered. The phrase is vague, but so is the common usage of words, especially words like "ought," and though it is difficult in border-line cases to say how much the agent could have been expected to foresee, it is easy enough to distinguish between some consequences which he could have been expected to foresee and some which he could not, and clear enough that he would be accused of not having done what he ought on account of the former but not on account of the latter. The definition is not intended to exclude cases where the only evidence of which he could be expected to take account is evidence which he actually had in mind when the emergency came or could obtain in the course of a very short time, for example in meeting a sudden attack, because immediate action of some sort was necessary.

I have not in all this attempted to give a definition of the different senses of "ought," but a rough explanation sufficient to distinguish them. The phrase I have used to explain the third sense of "ought," and perhaps also those used to explain the first and second senses, if taken as defining "ought," would be circular. For "preferable to choose" here really only means that the action is the one the agent *ought* to choose in preference to others. The first and the third alike depend directly on the same indefinable notion, as we shall see; with the second usage the question is a little more complicated.

A person who fails to do what he ought in the third sense is not necessarily morally to blame for this, since he may be honestly mistaken in the conclusions he drew from the evidence; but he will be either morally or intellectually to blame or both, that is he will have either willed more or less badly or reasoned more or less badly (including under this the omission of relevant points), or both. The difference between the three senses of "ought" may be illustrated in this way: If a motor knocks down and kills a man it is plain that the motorist ought not to have done what he did in the first sense of "ought," since it had unfortunate consequences (unless we argue that perhaps the death was a blessing in disguise); but it would be a matter for a court to decide whether he ought not to have done it in the third sense, with a view to determining whether damages were payable, while the question whether he did what he ought in the second sense would be considered by the court if it were a question of murder or manslaughter.

Corresponding to the three different senses of "ought" there are three different senses of "duty," "right," "wrong," which can easily be derived from the different senses of "ought," *mutatis mutandis.* Nor is the difference between the usage of the terms "ought," "right," "duty" of much philosophical importance. It does not at any rate point to a difference of fundamental concept at all. "The right action" is synonymous with the action which ought to be done, except that we should speak of God as doing what was right but should not apply to God the terms "duty" and "ought." This is because we do not admit the possibility of God's doing wrong. But "right" without the definite article has a wider significance. While an action which I ought to do or which it is my duty to do is always right, in the sense corresponding to the one of the three senses in which "ought" is being used in the given context, the converse does not hold. It is, for example, a right action to hand, with appropriate motives, a five-pound note to somebody to whom I owe five pounds, if I am not thereby violating any still more important obligation; but I cannot say that I ought to do this or that it is my duty to do this, because I should still be acting rightly if I handed him five pound notes instead, and two incompatible actions cannot both be duties. So we should say that I ought to pay the debt, but not that I ought to hand him a five-pound note. An act is thus right but not a duty, nor an act which we ought to do, where it is one of a number of alternative acts which are such that one ought to be done but there is no reason for preferring any one to any other of them. "Right," I think, means the same as "not wrong." We do not indeed usually use the term, "right," of indifferent acts, because we are not interested in these; but we should, if asked whether these were right or not right, admit that they were right. Ross, though he notes the distinction between "right" and "what ought to be done," in *The Right and the Good* [9] purposely chooses to use "right" as the adjective corresponding to "something that ought to be done"; but I do not intend to follow him in this, which, as he admits, is not the normal usage.

A "duty" is generally equivalent to an action or class of actions which ought to be done. But the term is not applied if (1) the main direct reason in favour of the action is its

---

[9] Pp. 3–4. In *Foundations of Ethics* (p. 44) he expresses the view that according to the normal usage of "right" any right act must be "a fulfilment of at least one claim upon us." But suppose somebody asks—Is it morally right to read a particular, harmless novel on Sunday? Anybody but a fanatical sabbatarian would surely answer—Yes, it is right, though no one would hold that there was a moral claim on us to read the novel.

conduciveness to the agent's own pleasure, and if (2) the action is in accord with the inclinations and present mood of the agent. If one of these two conditions is fulfilled but not the other, the action may, I think, still be called a duty. In general, however, the term is reserved for occasions on which we wish very specially to emphasize the moral aspect of an act. We are reluctant to describe acts of slight importance too readily as duties, thus cheapening the notion. It would not, however, be correct to say that "duty" was limited to the second sense of "ought," since we certainly admit that it is possible to make a mistake about one's duty.

In so far as the rightness or obligatoriness of an action depends on its consequences at all, whether we ought to perform an action in the first sense of "ought" will depend on the actual consequences, whether we ought to do it in the second sense on the consequences we judge likely, whether we ought to do it in the third sense neither on the actual consequences, nor on the consequences we judge likely, but on the consequences that relatively to our data really are likely. For to say that something is likely or probable is not merely to make a statement about my own or anybody else's subjective state. It has often been supposed that it is,[10] because I may truly say that something is improbable and yet it may really happen, or again I may judge something to be probable at one time and improbable at another and yet neither of the judgements may be wrong. If a person in July, 1940, judged that Germany would probably win the war, he is not proved to have been wrong by the fact that she did not do so. But judgements of probability cannot really be judgements about the subjective state of the person judging, for they are not reached by introspection but by considering the objective situation,

---

[10] See Prichard in *Duty and Ignorance of Fact*. Prichard's difficulties in this pamphlet seem to me to arise mainly from (a) ignoring the third sense of "right," (b) assuming that probability cannot be objective.

and I may make mistakes about estimating probability that are not mistakes about my subjective condition at all. If judgements of probability are judgements about one's own subjective state, it may be asked what they assert. They cannot be merely assertions about the degree of confidence with which the assertor entertains a proposition, if by "confidence" is meant confident feeling, because it is quite obvious that somebody, for example a sanguine gambler, may judge A to be less probable than B and yet feel more confident about A's happening than B, and it is still more obvious that he may feel a high degree of confidence concerning an event which he is quite wrong in judging probable at all. Nor can judgements of probability be merely assertions as to whether the assertor thinks something to be probable. The vicious circle is perfectly plain, and it is equally plain that a person may be mistaken in judging something probable and yet that it may be perfectly true that he thought it probable, indeed this must be true if he is even to make a mistake in judging the event probable. To be mistaken in judging it probable he must really judge it probable. Nor on a subjective view of probability do I see what possible sense could be given to statements attributing to an event a more or less definite degree of numerical probability. Some people have asserted that, when we judge an event probable, what we are really judging is that we shall act as if the event were going to occur; but owing to human folly or immorality people do not always act in accordance with their beliefs as to what is probable and, when I judge an event probable, I need not even anticipate that I will act in accord with my belief that it is probable. If I do anticipate this, it will only be because I have first concluded that the event is probable. After all it is surely quite clear that an event is not made probable, in any ordinary sense of the term, because we feel confident about it or think that it will happen or act as if it will.

Another objection is that, if we take a subjective view of probability, we shall have to say that all or most judgements of physical science or human history, since they are believed, or ought to be believed, by the person who makes them not to be quite certain but only probable, are or ought to be merely judgements about his state of mind at the time he makes them. Some philosophers have indeed held that all judgements, outside mathematics and formal logic, except those about one's own present state are uncertain; but surely they would not therefore be committed to saying that all these judgements are only about their own state of mind. That would commit them to solipsism. And if we do not go so far as these philosophers and admit that some judgements about physical objects and other human beings are certain, we still surely cannot say that, while the judgement that King George VI of England is alive at a particular date is about King George, the judgement that one of the Roman emperors was alive at a particular date, because it is only probable, only asserts that the man who makes it is in a certain state of mind now.

I therefore hold probability [11] to be an objective relation, whether definable or indefinable I need not discuss. This seems to me the only satisfactory way of reconciling (a), the fact that some events may truly be said, at different times, to be both probable and improbable, with (b), the fact that we can make mistakes about probability. The statement that A is probable is an incomplete statement like the statement that A is to the north or to the right, and there is no more difficulty in seeing how the statement that A is probable may be true in one case and false in another of the same event A than there is in seeing how the statement "Cambridge is to the north" may be true in London and false in Edinburgh. Nobody doubts on this ground that "Cambridge is to the north" can

---

[11] At least in the sense under discussion here.

describe an objective fact. "A is probable" makes no sense unless it is understood in relation to certain data, namely those available at the time the judgement is made, and therefore it may be true at one time and false at another according to differences in the data. It is obvious that in the light of probabilities we can determine with relative ease and even sometimes with fair certainty what we ought to do in the third sense of "ought" where it would be quite impossible to determine what we ought to do in the first, and that this goes far to explain the confidence which we often feel in ethical judgements, despite the multiplicity of possible consequences.

I must add, however, that, while I generally prefer to use "ought" in my third sense rather than in my first sense, what I "ought" to do in my first sense is still highly relevant to ethics. For it is only because, if I find out what is right in my third sense and act accordingly, I am more likely to approximate to what is right in my first sense, that I ought to do what is right in my third sense at all. We only consider what we ought to do in the third sense as a means to this approximation. We may compare the case of most theoretical knowledge. Outside mathematics, formal logic, and simple observations and memories, we have in theoretical knowledge to content ourselves with finding out what is probably, not what is certainly, true, yet the value of finding out what is probably true only lies in the fact that it is the best way of approximating to the objectively true, which is not itself probable or improbable but actual. In the theoretical sphere, if we accept what is really most probable relatively to our data rather than rush to conclusions without due consideration, we may err but at any rate we are likely to get nearer the truth than if we do not act in this reasonable way. We can be confident at least that we shall be far more often right, and that, where we err, we are likely to be less badly wrong and almost certain in most cases to have included some substantial truth in our error. The same applies in ethics. We cannot indeed hope to hit upon the absolutely best action to choose in any given situation, as in the realm of theory we cannot hope to hit upon the complete truth about any fact. But, as in the realm of theory we can arrive at some true propositions about something the nature of which is not wholly grasped, either scientifically or philosophically, so in the realm of ethics we may hope to make proper choices between alternatives and rightly prefer a to b, though we shall probably not think at all of the alternative action which it would be absolutely best to perform.

For what I have said about the first sense of "ought" should not suggest too extreme a scepticism. I do think that we can never be justified in believing a particular act to be the act which we ought to do in this sense of "ought"; but at least we can be sure that we are justified in believing it in the highest degree probable of many acts that they are much further than others from being what we ought to do in this sense. If the question is simply which to choose of a certain limited number of alternatives, there are many cases in which we can have at least a very well justified belief that it is right in my first sense to choose one kind of action rather than the others. For example, it is possible that, if I knocked somebody down because he criticised my philosophical arguments, it might by some indirect and unforeseeable concatenation of circumstances produce good effects which outbalanced the harm, but I should still be justified in strongly holding the opinion that it would be right even in my first sense of "right" to prefer to give a courteous answer; and this is unaffected by the fact that it is in the extremest degree unlikely that I should have hit upon the ideally and absolutely best way of treating the criticism. I can indeed not merely have a justifiable opinion, but know that, if I do knock the man down, I shall be committing an action that is very wrong in the first sense, as well as in the second and third senses, because even if owing to the strange concatenation of circumstances suggested it should turn out to be the right act *externally*, it is quite certain that, since I do not foresee these beneficent effects, I should not, if I did it, be acting in a right state of mind, and that is sufficient to prevent it from being right. But the most important point here is that the fact that the absolutely ideal action under the circumstances is not likely to occur to us need not make us sceptical as to our belief that certain actions under certain circumstances are preferable to certain others even in the first sense or that it is better to omit than to perform a certain action. The belief often does not amount to knowledge, but neither do many other beliefs on which the most timorous man is prepared to stake his life without a qualm; for example, that there is, in the absence of very special reasons for suspecting the contrary, no poison in his dinner. We may still go on fairly confidently with our moral judgements of preference. In no case may the ideal solution have occurred to us, but at least we may be confident that one particular solution is much better than another would be.

It may be objected that, when I talk about "ought" in the first and third usages, I am not really talking about anything moral at all. It is not my moral duty to choose rightly, though it is my moral duty to try to choose rightly, so you can only say that I *morally* ought to do something in the second sense of "ought," the sense according to which I am morally blame-worthy if I do not do what I ought. However, whether I am talking about the specifically moral "ought" or not, I am talk-ing about something which is extremely relevant to ethics and which is presupposed by the specifically moral sense of "ought." For I cannot decide what I ought to do in that sense without making up my mind what I ought to do in my third sense of "ought." I must first believe that an act is the prefer-able one to choose in view of the available data if I am to be

morally bound to do it. Some philosophers have spoken as if
the only proper sense of "ought" were the specifically moral
sense.[12] But I do not know what the criterion of "proper"
usage can be except the way in which educated people use a
term, and it is quite certain that "ought" is very widely and
constantly used in a sense which does not necessarily presuppose that it is morally wrong not to do what we ought. Indeed
it seems to me that in ordinary conversation it is more commonly used in such a way than in the specifically moral sense,
largely because people are shy of commenting to somebody
else about his morals. "You ought to have seen this film,"
"You ought to have moved your queen," even "Hitler ought
to have invaded England immediately after Dunkirk," are perfectly good English, and may be quite true statements even
though it is not considered a moral duty to see a film, to make
the right move in chess, and still less (by an Englishman) for
Hitler to invade England. The third sense of "ought" cannot,
however, be strictly described as a non-moral sense, nor for
that matter can the first sense of "ought." For to say that A
"ought" to do so-and-so in either of these senses entails that
under certain (factual) conditions he ought to do it in the
specifically moral sense of "ought." The proposition that a
man "ought" to do n in the first sense entails that he will do n
if he is adequately informed, wise and moral, and the proposition that a man "ought to do n" in the third sense entails
that he will do n if he is wise and moral. Similarly the proposition that he ought not (in the third sense) to have done what
he has done entails that he either has been unwise or has immorally neglected his duty. For I may fail to do what I
"ought" in that sense for two reasons, (a) because of a defect
of intelligence, (b) because of a defect of will. To say A

---

[12] Ross seems to take this view about "ought," though he admits that
"right" may legitimately be used in both senses (*Foundations of Ethics*, p.
55).

ought in that sense of "ought" to have done something which he did not do is to say that his action was inadequate or harmful through a defect in him, but to leave open (as we very often must in judging others) the question whether the defect was one of intelligence or of will. It implies that he either acted immorally or made a mistake. We are using "ought" in a completely non-moral sense only where we do not attach moral significance to the act at all, as in a game, or where we are considering not whether the act is right or wrong on the whole, but only whether it is so as means to a given end, which, as in the Hitler example, may be bad.

This brings out the point that "ought" really covers two different concepts, the concept of fittingness [13] and the concept of moral obligation. If I ought to do something there must be a certain relation between the action and its environment such that the action is fitting, appropriate, suitable, and its omission unfitting, inappropriate, unsuitable. This in itself is, however, a different concept from the concept of a moral obligation which we must fulfil or be guilty of sin, yet the latter concept must always be based on the former. Sin cannot occur unless our act is inappropriate in some way to the situation or at least we believe it to be so. This is obviously true, though we generally express it by using some stronger word than "unfitting" or "inappropriate." Nobody would in ordinary conversation describe a brutal murder as "unfitting"; the murder would no doubt be unfitting, but the word is not felt to be strong enough. It is, however, very convenient for philosophical purposes to have a single word which covers all degrees, so I shall follow Broad in using "fitting" for this purpose, as a physicist in defiance of ordinary usage employs the word "heat" to cover temperatures far below zero. But this concept of fittingness by no means exhausts the significance

---

[13] This term is borrowed from Professor Broad.

of "ought." There is the further concept of strictly moral obligation. We feel that we are under binding laws which we cannot break without being ourselves evil in a more serious and quite different way from that in which pain is evil. We feel that it is not merely an interesting fact that A is an unfitting action in circumstances B, C, D, but one which has a claim to authority over us. This is not to define "moral obligation," but to clarify the distinction between it and mere fittingness. Even if it is held that we are morally obliged to do what is most fitting, it must be admitted that the two concepts are distinct. But it is not the case that we are always morally obliged to do what is most fitting. For, although A is really the most fitting action relatively to all the circumstances, or even to those which are known to the agent, he may through ignorance or misjudgement not be aware of this, and in that case he will not be under a moral obligation to do A. Further, we can apply the term "fitting" in regard to matters which are not subject to volition, while we cannot apply the term "morally obligatory" in that way. Finally, certain actions are fitting simply because they are conducive to the agent's happiness, yet it may at least be doubted whether this is a sufficient ground to make them morally obligatory, which at any rate proves the two concepts not to be identical, even if we should finally reject the doubt and decide that they are morally obligatory after all. "Fittingness" stands for a relation between an action and its environment, moral obligation is something analogous to an imperative on the agent. So we have at least three different and apparently fundamental ethical concepts —goodness, fittingness, and moral obligation—the relations of which to explore.

It may be objected that the concept of moral obligation in so far as it goes beyond fittingness is theological, as has often been said to be the case with the allied concept of sin, and that therefore as long as we are dealing simply with ethics apart from any theological assumptions we ought not to introduce it. But it is certainly a part of the moral consciousness, if anything is, that we are under binding obligations, and if we took the notion away from ethics there would be little left of ethics. If this concept does necessarily involve theology, then we can argue from ethics to the existence of God. As I have tried to make clear earlier, we must in any case not reverse the argument and say that we must first believe in theology before we can rightly believe that we are under moral obligations. We are directly and certainly conscious of moral obligation, and if that is disputed there can be little ground for a theology which would re-establish ethics. If belief in a good God—and a God that was not good would assuredly provide no basis for ethics—is to be established by argument, the argument must already presuppose ethical concepts and propositions. On the other hand, if it is claimed that we can be immediately aware without argument of such a being independently of the ethical consciousness and deduce our ethics from the nature of the being thus intuited, we are basing the more certain on the less certain, since we are appealing to an intuition which is, at the best, less, not more, certain than are our clearest ethical intuitions. Even if belief in God were based exclusively not on our reason or intuition at all but on the revelation of Christ, we may reply that there would be little ground indeed for believing in the revelation if we did not assume at least that Christ was good, and we could not assume this without trusting to our own power of ethical discrimination. Even if theology be the *ratio essendi* of ethics, it is certainly not its *ratio cognoscendi*. In order to be aware that we are under moral obligations we need not first come to know or believe anything about God, even that there is a God. This will be the case even if it should turn out that some of the concepts of ethics—we have seen above [14] that this cannot be

---

[14] V. pp. 106 ff.

the case with all—cannot be analysed or at least grasped adequately without a reference to God.

My first and third senses of "ought" express fittingness, not merely fittingness for a particular end (as with Kant's "hypothetical imperatives"), though I do not deny that "ought" is also used in that sense, but fittingness in regard to the situation as a whole. But with the first sense the situation is viewed in abstraction from any imperfections in the agent's knowledge and beliefs, and with the third sense the situation is viewed in abstraction, not from all such imperfections, but from those due to his mistakes, negligence, or prejudice. The first and third senses give the act which of those possible is the most fitting if we take into account everything except the above circumstances. The second sense gives the action which is fitting in relation to the situation as the agent views it and at the same time the action which is morally obligatory. I think it to be a true synthetic *a priori* proposition that it is morally obligatory for an agent to do A where he thinks A the most fitting action in his power and where it is both possible for him to do and also possible for him not to do A. There would be serious difficulties and disputes about the definition of "possible," but these are beyond the scope of this book; and even the determinist would admit some sense of "possible" in which it is possible for a man to act differently from the way in which he actually does act. In order to decide which action is most fitting the agent cannot first take into account his belief as to which is most fitting, for this is not yet formed, therefore he must be asking himself which action he ought to do in my third sense of "ought," not in my second sense which already presupposes that he has made up his mind as to which act is the fitting one to do. Now suppose he is mistaken and acts according to his false belief. He can be said to have done what he morally ought to do, but he cannot be said to have done what he ought in the sense of what is most fitting to the situation. It might be argued that he has still done the most fitting, or the least unfitting, act in his power, for if he had done the act which was externally the most fitting, he would have done it from a bad motive or in a bad state of mind, and it therefore would not have been really the most fitting action. In such a situation, since there is no absolutely fitting action which he could do, the question is which is the least unfitting. But, bad as it is to do what one believes to be wrong, it may be on occasion less inappropriate to the situation that somebody should do this than that he should do a terribly harmful act which he erroneously thinks right. To make this clear by an example, let us suppose that on September 1, 1939, Hitler really thought it his duty to order the invasion of Poland. It would still have been less inappropriate to the situation that Hitler should have neglected to obey his conscience on this occasion, even through bad motives such as laziness or coward-ice, than that he should have obeyed it with all the terrible effects in suffering and moral evil that the war brought in its wake. We cannot therefore say that it is always most fitting to do what one thinks most fitting, but one may still be able to say that it is always morally obligatory to do so. To keep the peace, even believing this to be wrong, would have been less unfitting than to break the peace believing it to be right. Yet the latter, and not the former, was Hitler's duty in my second sense of "duty," if he held that belief, though no doubt he violated his duty in all senses in getting into a state in which it was possible for him to hold (if he ever did hold) the belief. I think, therefore, that the second sense of "ought" differs from the other two in that to say something ought to be done in this sense is to make no statement about the real, as opposed to the believed, fittingness of the action. It also differs in that it can be applied only to actions. The first and third can also be applied to emotions or opinions, whereas it cannot be said that a person "ought" in my second sense to have an emotion or opinion, though it can be said that he ought (in this sense of "ought") to take steps to develop right emotions and opinions.

What is it that I ought to do in any or all the different senses of "ought"? Ought I to act from a certain motive, or is it only true that I ought to act or "set myself to act"? Ross has maintained that it is never the case that I ought to act from a certain motive, since "ought" implies "can" and it is not in my power to remove or alter a desire at once at the time I have it.[15] It is in my power to take steps which will affect the desires I shall feel at some future time, but this will be too late to influence the motive of the action I am doing now, though it may influence future motives. The same applies to the sense of duty as a motive, even if that is distinguished from any desire. Ross therefore held in *The Right and the Good*[16] that what we ought to do is only to produce certain results, so that if I return a book to a friend and it reaches him I shall have done what I ought, however bad my motives and however carelessly I packed it, while if it fails to reach him through an unforeseen accident I shall, however good my motives and however carefully I packed it, not have done what I ought. But before he published *Foundations of Ethics* Ross was convinced by some of the objections to this view, so then he substituted for it the view that what we ought to do is, not to produce a given result or perform a given physical act, but merely to set ourselves to do so. He, however, still maintained the view that it was not our duty to do, or to set ourselves to do, anything from a given motive, since our motives are not directly under the control of the will.[17] But it still seems paradoxical to say that I have done what I ought if I either give or "set myself" to persuade the board of examiners

---

[15] *The Right and the Good*, pp. 4-5.
[16] Id., pp. 42 ff.
[17] V. *Foundation of Ethics*, Chap. VI.

to give a candidate who deserves it a third-class mark not because I think he deserves it but because I dislike him, or if I set myself to pay my debts because I want to ingratiate myself with my creditor in order to obtain his help in robbing a third party. We must not indeed exaggerate the paradoxical character of what Ross is saying: he would admit that it is morally bad to do these things from such motives, and that I ought to try to reform myself so that on future occasions I shall have better motives. But, if I acted in the way mentioned, it would seem obvious to most people not only that I had done something morally bad but that I had done something wrong. They would admit that I had neglected my duty.

Yet Ross's argument must somehow be met if we are to maintain that it is ever a duty to act from a given motive. I thought at one time that I could refute his argument by pointing out that "motive" is not equivalent just to "desire" but to "desire *qua* cause of an act" I then contended that, though it is impossible for me to remove a desire except by a somewhat lengthy process, I can still be said to be able to control my motives because I can prevent a desire from causing me to act and so from becoming a motive. But this oversimplifies the situation. If I can control my acts at all, it must indeed be possible for me sometimes at the moment of acting to prevent a certain desire from causing me to act. For I choose to act in a different way from that to which the desire points. But what about the case Ross has in mind where two different desires would each produce the same act? Supposing I perform the act, is it in my power at the time to decide which of the desires is to cause it? It is difficult to see how it could be, for it can only be caused by a past (though very recently past) state, not a present state, and I cannot now alter the past. Further, the act which I will is *ex hypothesi* the same whichever desire caused it, therefore it is difficult to see what difference there would be between choosing to act on one and choosing to act on the other except that I should feel differently, and it is generally admitted, as Ross urges, that my feelings cannot be changed immediately by an act of will but require for their alteration a longer process.

In order to deal with this question I think the best course is to ask: What then ought I to do if I believe that n is the right act but the state of my desires is such as to make me inclined to do n from a wrong motive? Clearly I ought to take special care in deciding whether n really is the right act, since there will be a great danger of my desires prejudicing me in the matter, and it may even for that reason be best to postpone acting. On these grounds Plato laid down the rule that we ought to avoid punishing somebody while we are angry. But postponement of a decision may sometimes be disastrous. Suppose I am convinced after adequate consideration that n is right and that it would be foolish to wait longer before doing n, but suppose also that the bad motive is more clearly present in my mind than the good. (It cannot be alone present, otherwise I should not seriously ask the question what I ought to do at all.) Clearly it is now my duty to do n, and it will not be possible for me to prevent myself feeling a certain satisfaction at this for wrong reasons, but I can at least direct my attention to the aspects of the question which make the action my duty rather than to those which give me illicit satisfaction. Modern psychology has shown that it is best to recognise frankly that the less desirable tendency is present, but it is clearly also true that I ought not to rest in the enjoyment of this but recognise it as something to be fought against. At any rate it is clear that, although we cannot alter our desires at a moment's notice, we can control our attention and therefore our present state of mind to some extent, so that there seems to me to be no adequate ground for saying that it can only be my duty to act, not to act in a certain state of mind. A state of mind in which I will to punish A but attend mainly to the pleasure I obtain from doing so or to the harm A has done *me* is radically different from a state of mind in which I will to punish A but direct my attention to the good reasons for doing so, even if I cannot now help feeling the pleasure (whatever I might have done earlier to avoid getting into this malevolent frame of mind). The morally important thing is, not how I feel, but how my will is directed. If it be objected that some time, however little, will elapse between my willing to attend and my actually attending, it may equally be said that some time will elapse between my willing to perform and my actually performing a physical act. If, as in Prichard's *Duty and Ignorance of Fact* and Ross's *Foundations of Ethics*, what a man ought to do is held to be simply to "set himself" to effect a certain change, this is already to admit that his duty is to change his state of mind in a certain way. So why not also admit a duty to change it in the way I suggest, since he would thereby, as Ross and Prichard both admit, make his action intrinsically better than it would otherwise be?

So the answer to the question whether it is our duty only to do something or to do it from a particular motive seems to depend on whether we mean by "motive" (1) a desire causing action or (2) circumstances relevant to the action on which our attention is fixed at the time of action. In the former case we perhaps cannot say that it is our duty at the time of action to act from one motive rather than another, for, since a cause must lie in the past, that would be saying that it was our duty to alter the past. But we can say that it is our duty to deflect our attention in such a way as to weaken the desire by attending to circumstances which would discourage rather than encourage it. In the latter case we can say that it is our duty at the time to act from a certain motive, as truly as we can say that it is our duty to act, or set ourselves to act, at all. It may be contended in regard to acting and acting from a given motive alike that they are duties which never refer to the present but always only to the (very) immediate future, since all causation takes time. The recognition that the exhortation to act from good motives is an exhortation not so much to cultivate certain feelings directly as to attend to certain features of the act and of its consequences in preference to others also enables one to reconcile the duty to act from good motives with a new line of argument introduced by Ross in *Foundations of Ethics.*[18] He says there: "When we ask what it is that makes an act my duty we are asking what is the *distinctive* feature of that act that makes it and not some other to be my duty. Now, *whichever* of two or more acts I decide to be my duty, I shall do it (if I carry out my intention) from the sense of duty. The motive will be the same whichever I do; the motive therefore can be no part of that which makes the one act my duty while the others are not, since the same motive will be the motive of whichever act I do. . . . What is it to which we in fact find ourselves attending when we are trying to discover our duty in some situation? Is it not clear that what we attend to is the nature of the possible acts, considered apart from the motive from which we should do them —their tendency to affect the welfare of other people in this way or in that, their quality as fulfilments of promise or breaches of promise, and the like?" I certainly agree that, except for some indirect reason, consideration of my motives as desires does not help me to find out what is my duty. On the whole the objective features of an action are what we should consider, and the duty to act from a good motive, in so far as it can be contrasted with the duty of acting as such, seems to lie in attending to some of these rather than to others.

Ross also argues that, if it is my duty to do act A from the sense of duty, we must admit that it is my duty to do A from the sense that it is my duty to do A from the sense that it is my duty to do A and so on *ad infinitum*, thus involving a vicious infinite regress.[19] However, it seems to me that in the sentence "It is my duty to do A from a sense of duty" "duty" is usually being used in two different ways. Where it occurs first in the sentence, it is used in my second sense, that is, to mean that it is morally obligatory to act in a certain way; where it occurs for the second time, it is used in my third sense. The sentence then will mean that it is a moral obligation to do A because you believe A to be objectively fitting relatively to the available data, and therefore there will be no contradiction in saying that it is my duty to do A from the sense of duty, even though we mean by the latter the sense that it is our duty to do it *simpliciter* (not from a sense of duty), because "duty" means something different in the two cases. But even if it were held that I ought to act from a sense that it was morally obligatory (not merely from a sense that it was fitting) to act in this way, it would not necessarily follow that I ought to act from a sense that it was morally obligatory to act from a sense that it was morally obligatory to act in this way, still less from a sense that it was morally obligatory to act from a sense that it was morally obligatory to act from a sense that it was morally obligatory to act in this way. It may be doubted whether anybody has such a sense at all, and certainly nobody will have it but a philosopher! These conclusions, it seems to me, would only follow if we assumed that it was my duty always to do whatever I did from a sense of duty, and this Ross himself does not hold. If it is only my duty to do some of the things that I do from a sense of duty, it may well be my duty to do A from a sense of duty without its being also my duty to have this motive itself from a sense of duty and so on *ad infinitum*.

---

[19] *The Right and the Good*, p. 5; *Foundations of Ethics*, pp. 116 ff.

Ross's argument seems to depend also on supposing that there is a contradiction between saying that it is my duty to do A *simpliciter* and saying that it is my duty to do A from a sense of duty. But doing A is a genus of which the various species are doing A from the various kinds of possible motive, and if it is my duty to do an action which falls in one of the species it is *ipso facto* my duty to do an action which falls in the genus. The latter assertion, so far from contradicting the former, is entailed by it. There can be no contradiction in saying that I ought to do an action of genus A from the sense that it is my duty to do an action of this genus. It might after all be true both that I ought to pay a particular debt and that I ought to pay it from certain motives rather than from others. That the statement that I ought to pay the debt does not give a complete description of what I ought to do in this matter does not prevent it from being a true statement as far as it goes. However, as what I have said before suggests, the truth probably is, not that we ought to act from a sense of duty in the sense of our act being determined by the desire to do our duty, but in the sense that we ought to act with our attention directed to those characteristics of the act which make it a duty rather than to others. For example, in paying our debts we ought to attend rather to the fact that we owe the money than to the fact that we shall be summoned if we do not pay them, or shall make it easier for ourselves to obtain improper favours from our creditors if we do.

It follows that in all the senses of "ought" discussed what we ought to do is not merely to act, but to act in a certain state of mind or with a certain direction of attention. I therefore cannot agree with Ross's view in *The Right and the Good* [20] that what ought to be done is never morally good. It is morally good to act in the fitting way with my attention

---

[20] P. 4.

directed towards the right aspects of the act, especially where there is a temptation to do the opposite. And to do so is both fitting and, if I believe it to be the fitting course, obligatory. An immoral action, on the other hand, is from the nature of the case one not done with a right direction of attention, and so even if it turned out by accident to be in its external features the most beneficial act possible it would not be right. As regards mistakes I should say that if I mistakenly believe that *a* is my duty (in my first or my third sense), when *a* is really wrong, it is impossible for me to perform the right (fitting) action (in the sense in question), though it is possible for me to perform the morally obligatory act (second sense of "duty" or "right"). For if I do the act which I think right, it will for external reasons be unfitting, and if I perform the act which is really externally right I shall be performing it in a state of mind which is unfitting.

CHAPTER V

An Analysis of Good in Terms of Ought

Having distinguished the different senses of "good" and "ought" as far as necessary, we can now consider whether it is possible to define the one ethical concept in terms of the other. What Moore was attacking when he insisted that "good" could not be defined was any attempt to define it in purely non-ethical terms. The objections to such attempts are not valid against an attempt to define it by means of other ethical concepts or to give it a mixed definition consisting partly of ethical and partly of psychological terms. This proceeding would not be open to the charge of explaining away or destroying the specific character of ethical ideas; and it is such a definition that I propose now to attempt. I have indeed insisted that at least one ethical concept must be unanalysable, but that concept may perhaps not be the concept of good. Now the only other ethical term besides "good" which could be plausibly claimed to be fundamental is "ought." We have, however, seen that this term expresses two different fundamental concepts, fittingness and moral obligation. Let us try first whether we can define "good" in terms of "ought" as standing for the former, and then consider the notion of moral obligation afterwards. I do not indeed see any prospect of defining "good" in terms of fittingness alone— that could only be done if goodness and fittingness were simply synonymous—but it might be definable in terms of fittingness together with some psychological concept.

The question at issue between naturalist and non-naturalist is not whether "good" is ever used in a non-naturalist sense, but whether it is always so used. Now the sense of "good" which is usually being considered when we ask whether "good" is or is not analysable is that usually distinguished from others by the use of the phrases "intrinsically good," "good as an end," "good-in-itself." It is this sense of "good" that we shall discuss. When we have arrived at a definition, we can try to derive from it definitions of any other non-naturalist senses of "good." The term "intrinsically good" may be technical, but in so far as there is no point in anything being good as a means unless something is good as an end it is presupposed in all commonsense talk about what is good.

The definition I shall suggest will be partly in ethical and partly in psychological terms. Provided irreducible ethical terms are introduced at all, even if they do not make up the whole of the definition, this will save it from the charge of being naturalist. I do not claim orginality for the definition; [1] if I show any originality at all, it will be in the consequences that I deduce from it. Now, strange to say, the definition is one actually suggested by Moore himself. For he suggests that we might take as a synonym for "good" as applied to an experience the phrase "worth having for its own sake." [2] To say this is not necessarily inconsistent with the view that good is indefinable, for there might be various phrases which could be properly used as verbal synonyms in order to help people to see more clearly what is meant by a term without being themselves eligible as definitions of the term. It might be the case that "worth" in "worth having for its own sake" could itself only be defined in terms of "good," so that the phrase would be quite useless as a definition of

---

[1] V., for example, Osborne, *The Philosophy of Value*, pp. 93 ff.
[2] Proceedings of Arist. Soc., Supp. Vol. XI, pp. 122 ff.

the latter, and yet it might be appropriately used to help some people to become clear as to what they meant by "good," and especially to distinguish the sense under discussion from other senses of "good." However I think that in fact "worth having for its own sake" can be analysed in a way which does not make it a vicious circle to use the phrase as a definition of "good"; but, before I propound my analysis, I should like the reader to consider carefully whether the phrase "an intrinsically good experience" is or is not the exact equivalent of "an experience worth having for its own sake." In this definition, unlike the naturalist definitions, it seems clear both that the *definiens* and the *definiendum* are coextensive, and that this is necessarily so. It seems clear that there could not be an experience which was intrinsically good that was yet not worth having for its own sake, nor an experience which was worth having for its own sake that was not intrinsically good. This seems to me not merely a contingent fact but a logical necessity. Now it may well be the case that, say, A B entails and is entailed by C, and yet that A B is not a definition of C; consequently it is impossible strictly to prove that anything is a definition of anything else. So in the present case it is open to anybody to maintain that besides the characteristic expressed by the words "worth having for its own sake" there is another, indefinable characteristic, goodness. He should maintain this, if he thinks he can discern such a characteristic which always necessarily accompanies, but is different from, the characteristic of being worth having for its own sake. But I am not clear that I can discern any such characteristic, and I should point to the fact that, when in ordinary conversation we wish to convey exactly the meaning of the term "intrinsically good" to a person not familiar with it, we should most naturally use the phrase in question. "Worth having for its own sake" seems to be in fact just the phrase which the man in the street, when he is talking about experiences, would use to express what the philosopher calls "intrinsically" as distinct from "instrumentally good."

But, while "worth having for its own sake" is equivalent to "intrinsically good" when applied to an experience, there is an objection to taking it as equivalent to "intrinsically good" without qualification. It is this: though it is often held that experiences are the only things which can be intrinsically good, we must not define "intrinsically good" in a way which would make it a verbal contradiction to say of anything but an experience that it was intrinsically good. To say that the State is good-in-itself or to say that beautiful things are good-in-themselves may be wrong but is not verbally self-contradictory. Now on the definition of "intrinsically good" suggested it would be verbally self-contradictory or meaningless, because experiences are the only kind of things that we can be said to "have" in this sense of "have," [3] though there are other senses of "have" in which it is possible to have, for example, beautiful objects. But this does not prevent the definition from being adequate when we are talking of a person's experiences as such. What is an experience which is worth having for its own sake? It is one that it is reasonable to choose for its own sake, or that a man ought, other things being equal, to bring into existence for its own sake. Now these phrases themselves are not by the very meaning of the words limited to experiences. So, if we are looking for a definition which will not be confined to experiences, we might define "intrinsically good" as "worth choosing or producing for its own sake." However, though this definition will mostly serve, there may be cases where it cannot well be applied, and it is difficult to find a single form of words which is always applicable. But we might adopt a technical term and define "good" as what ought to be the object of a pro

---

[3] As Moore points out, id., p. 124.

attitude (to use Ross's word). "Pro attitude" is intended to cover any favourable attitude to something. It covers, for instance, choice, desire, liking, pursuit, approval, admiration. The variety of these attitudes would go far to explain how it is that "good" may be used in so many different senses. "Worth having" as applied to experiences seems to mean that the experience in itself is a suitable one to choose for one's own or to give to somebody else, and to entail that it should be welcomed and not avoided or deplored. It may be reasonable to renounce or avoid it on account of some bad consequences which it may have or for the sake of obtaining something still better, but as an experience it is not only desired but desirable in the absence of any positive reason against it. So we have obtained a definition of "intrinsically good" in terms of "ought," and while the phrase "worth having for its own sake" can without verbal contradiction be applied only to experiences, the definition now given can be applied more widely, if there are indeed things other than experiences which are good in the sense under discussion. When something is intrinsically good, it is (other things being equal) something that on its own account we ought to welcome, rejoice in if it exists, seek to produce if it does not exist.[4] We ought to approve its attainment, count its loss a deprivation, hope for and not dread its coming if this is likely, avoid what hinders its production, etc. A definition of this sort is indicated by the very common tendency to take "desirable" as a synonym for "good" in ordinary speech. I do not think myself that in most cases where "good" is used it is best defined in terms of desire, but it may well be that it is best defined in terms of some similar attitude. We must, however, unlike Mill, remember that "desirable" signifies what "ought to be desired," not just "what is desired"; and this same point will apply, what-

---

[4] I think it to be a synthetic *a priori* proposition that we ought to welcome what is worth producing for its own sake, etc.

ever mental attitude we select for our definition in preference to desire. It need not always be the same attitude. When we call something good, we may be thinking sometimes rather of the fact that we ought to welcome it, sometimes rather of the fact that we ought to seek it, etc. But we can see various attitudes I have mentioned to have something in common that is opposed to the common element in condemning, shunning, fearing, regretting, etc., which would supply the corresponding definition of "bad." The former may be called pro attitudes, the latter anti attitudes. The former are positive and favourable to their objects, the latter negative and hostile.

But what is the sense of "ought" when we say we ought to have a pro attitude to what is good and an anti attitude to what is bad? In the last chapter I have distinguished the concept of fittingness from the concept of moral obligation. It is clearly the former which is involved here, not the latter, though there may be other senses of "good" in which the latter comes to the fore. When we are saying that something is worth pursuing for its own sake, we are not saying that one morally ought to pursue it. That may be impossible for a particular person and therefore not morally obligatory. Nor are we necessarily even saying that a man morally ought to pursue it if he can and if there is no positive objection to his doing so. Most [5] pleasant experiences are worth having for their own sake, but, if the experience is merely a pleasure of an innocent but not very elevated kind, most people would hold that I should not be morally to blame for deliberately neglecting to obtain that experience for myself. Now this, whether a right judgement or not, is certainly not verbally inconsistent with saying that pleasure is intrinsically good. As I have pointed out, the word "ought" (without its strictly moral implications) is constantly used in such cases, for

---

[5] Not all, for example, not drunkenness or sadism.

example, "You ought to have seen that film." It does seem clear that, when I say that such a pleasant experience is intrinsically good, I am asserting that it is preferable to have it rather than not, or that, other things being equal, I ought to choose it in my first or third sense of "ought." Whether I should be morally to blame or not for declining to choose to have it when I could do so without corresponding harm, at any rate it would be fitting, rational, desirable for me to choose the experience in question. If we mean by "good" what ought to be desired, approved, or admired, it seems still more obvious to me that we are thinking of "ought" in the sense in which it signifies fittingness rather than moral obligation. For I cannot by an act of will desire, approve, or admire something. Yet it is perfectly plain that there is a sense in which it can be said that I ought to have these emotional attitudes to certain things—and not merely that I ought to cultivate them as far as I can. "Ought" here signifies that these emotional attitudes are fitting. It is more appropriate, or fitting, to feel disgust than pleasure at cruelty, more appropriate to desire reconciliation than revenge, to admire fidelity than clever cheating, to feel aesthetic emotions on contemplating great works of art than not to do so. When we say this, I do not think we are directly considering whether the person who has the appropriate or inappropriate feelings has done what he morally ought or not. His feelings are still unfitting even if he was so badly brought up that he could not be expected to see their wrongness or try to improve his feelings. He may not be to blame for them, but that does not make them fitting. If it did, the fact that he had been badly brought up would not be so deplorable; indeed if his bringing up did not produce unfitting feelings and actions he could not be said to have been "badly brought up." Similarly an action may be condemned as unfitting in the circumstances under which it is done even if the person who does it has not the intelligence to foresee the likelihood of the consequences which make it unfitting, provided only these consequences were humanly foreseeable.

So we are in the definition of "good" using "ought," not in the second sense, earlier distinguished,[*] to signify moral obligation, but to signify fittingness. We may therefore define "good" as "fitting object of a pro attitude," either without qualification (my first sense of "ought"), or as qualified by the terms "so far as is in the light of the available evidence foreseeable" (my third sense of "ought"). (While we could never be confident that any complete action we did was one we ought to do in the first sense, we can be confident or even know that we ought to treat certain objects as ends-in-themselves, have certain mental attitudes, and feel certain emotions in this sense of "ought.") When I say this I think I am giving a strict definition of what "good" means, or at least approximating as closely as a philosophical analysis ever could to an exact definition of a commonsense term. I am not merely saying what being good entails, still less amending the commonsense meaning so as to fit in with my philosophy. The position is complicated by the variety of the different senses of "good"; but I think it is a strong point of my definition that all the different senses can be brought under it or at least closely related to it. In its primary sense as intrinsically good, "good," I think, usually means "worth producing or pursuing for its own sake, other things being equal." To apply "good" to something is to say of this that it is fitting, other things being equal, to bring it into existence. That, as we have seen, is shown by the naturalness of the equation of "good" with "worth having" when applied to experiences. It has been several times proposed to define "good" as "desirable," meaning by this word not, as Mill apparently did in a famous (or notorious?) passage,

---

[*] V. above, pp. 120-21.

"actual object of desire" but "fitting object of desire." But, if "desire" means a certain uneasy emotion, it is not true that we ought to feel desire towards whatever is intrinsically good. The less we feel this emotion towards what we cannot obtain, or in any degree bring about, however good that object may be, the better on the whole. For such desire will only make us less happy and distract us from our other activities without doing any good. On the other hand, if desire means something more than an uneasy emotion, it becomes a striving to pursue and bring about the existence of its object, and if so the definition in terms of desire merges into the definition in terms of pursuit. This is in fact, I think, what we almost always mean when we say that something is desirable; we do not mean that we ought to feel a certain emotion towards it, but that the object is worth producing or pursuing. It is therefore better to say this frankly in our definition than to use a word which is more ambiguous. There may well be cases in which "good" is used to signify rather "what it is fitting to desire" than "what it is fitting to produce or pursue," but I think they will be rare. I am in this objecting to "desirable" as the standard definition; but "fitting object of pursuit," though a great improvement as a definition, cannot itself be substituted for "good" in all cases even of what is pronounced intrinsically good.

Among the things which are spoken of as "intrinsically good" are actions. Now in this case I do not think that people are generally using the term in the same sense as when they use it, for example, of pleasant experiences. We regard, for example, a particular act of self-sacrifice as intrinsically good. Do we mean to say that it is fitting that the person who makes the sacrifice should choose, produce, or pursue it for its own sake quite apart from consequences? Surely not. That would lead to irrational asceticism. To sacrifice himself when it does no good to anyone is not something which a man ought to choose to do. The self-sacrificing action does not seem to be intrinsically good in the sense in which, for example, innocent pleasures, aesthetic experiences, personal affection, intellectual activity are held to be so. If it were, ought we not to spend most of our time torturing ourselves in order to realize the value of self-sacrifice, since moral values are generally admitted to be higher than happiness and their absence in beings capable of them a worse evil than pain? But intrinsic goodness as applied to actions may still be analysed in terms of fittingness, provided the psychological term of the analysis is different. Now we certainly regard righteous acts of self-sacrifice as admirable in themselves even if they fail to achieve the desired result. So I suggest that we usually mean by "good actions" simply actions that it is fitting to admire or approve. This is certainly not the usual meaning of "intrinsically good" in the earlier cases. A pleasure, however innocent, is not something to be admired, though it is something to be liked and, other things being equal, pursued.

But we must add a qualification and say "morally admired" or "morally approved." For we may also admire or approve a cleverness which does not display moral qualities, though our admiration even for the cleverness in itself is lessened if it displays immoral ones. Nor must we use "admired" or "approved" here to stand for "judged good," since in that case we should be guilty of a vicious circle. The word must, in the analysis given, stand for an emotion or a state of mind tinged with emotional qualities. I do not wish to discuss the psychological question whether moral emotion is a single emotion or a class or blend of emotions; but it does seem to me that there is something specific about this kind of admiration which distinguishes it from other kinds. And it is quite clear that there are certain actions to which this kind of feeling is the appropriate reaction, as sympathy is to suffering and certain aesthetic experiences to a great drama. There is, however, a curious point here to note in passing: with persons other than the agent himself the appropriate reaction is admiration; but with the agent himself it is not. A man should not admire himself. Such a difference between the emotion appropriate to a quality in another person and that appropriate to the same quality in oneself is, however, not unparalleled; sympathy and pity are appropriate emotions when directed towards another's pain, but one should try to avoid self-pity, and it is doubtful whether there is any sense in talking about feeling sympathy with oneself. Moral disapproval or condemnation is, on the other hand, a fitting emotion for both the agent and others when directed towards morally evil actions, but most moral disapproval of oneself feels so very different from most moral disapproval of others that it is appropriately designated by a different word, "shame." (We may indeed feel shame for the actions of another person; but it is clear that this feeling is derivative from the feeling one has for one's own wrong acts and moral defects, and only arises because through sympathy we put ourselves in the place of the person who has done wrong.)

If we are not willing to regard moral admiration as a specific emotion, we can still retain the principle of the definition by defining "good actions" in the moral sense as actions more or less admirable on account of certain volitional characteristics. They will be those actions that show a direction of the will to right ends and a persistence in face of temptation in doing what is thought right. In that case moral admiration and other kinds of admiration will be distinguished, not by the way they feel but by their objects. Clever or beautiful pieces of work would also be fitting objects of admiration but for a different reason, not so connected with the will, and we should therefore not speak of moral admiration of them. In any case the term "admirable" is wider than "morally admirable," so this already gives us two different senses of "good," one wider, one narrower, "admirable" and "morally admirable," besides the previous sense discussed in which it stands for an object which it is fitting to pursue, promote, or choose for its own sake.

These three different senses will have two very important points in common: (a) they define "good" in terms of fittingness together with a psychological factor, (b) the latter is a "pro attitude," though the pro attitude is different. The attitudes are, in a very definite sense, favourable to the object towards which they are directed. That "intrinsically good" should be used in different senses not clearly distinguished is, when the senses have so much in common, not very surprising. My view here bears a certain similarity to that of Ross, though it was reached independently before I knew that he had also made the distinction in question. Ross distinguishes two senses of "good": in one sense the term applies to certain moral dispositions and actions, and intellectual and aesthetic activities, and in the other to pleasure. In the former sense the term "may be paraphrased by saying that they are fine or admirable activities of the human spirit, and by adding that they are good in such a way that any one who has them or does them is to that extent being good himself. Pleasure is never good in this, which I should call the most proper sense of 'good.' But the pleasures of others (except those which are immoral) are good in a secondary sense, viz. that they are morally worthy or suitable objects of satisfaction." [1] The differences between us are, however, greater than appear at first sight.

(1) Ross holds that his first sense of "good," though capable of being "paraphrased" in the way given, is indefinable, while I have put forward "fitting object of admiration" as a definition of this sense of "good." I do not know how to decide

---

[1] *Foundations of Ethics*, p. 283.

between the two views except by asking myself whether I can form a distinct idea of a characteristic, goodness, common to morally admirable actions over and above the characteristic of being a fitting object of moral admiration, and I do not think I can. It may be retorted that, if an action is to be worthy of moral admiration, this must be because of something in the action itself. But this, though true, need not imply that there must be a single quality, goodness, over and above both the psychological qualities which make the action morally admirable and the non-natural characteristics of being an action which ought to be admired and one which ought to be done. There are various psychological characteristics, for example the direction of the will to a certain end, and there are the non-natural characteristics, based on these, of being an action which ought to be done [8] and of being a fitting object of admiration, but besides these there is no further quality of goodness which I can detect. Ross says that "admiration" is "an emotion accompanied by the thought that that which is admired is good," and concludes that it would therefore be a vicious circle to say that anything was good if we meant by this only that it was worthy of admiration. We admire something only because we first think it good, and therefore, he holds, we cannot base the definition of "good" on the concept of admiration. Now we certainly may sometimes admire something because we first think it good, but this is not incompatible with my definition. If we define "good" as "worthy of admiration," the sentence will still make sense, for I might well admire something just because I thought it worthy to be admired. But this is not the only proper ground of admiration. We must guard against a confusion here: the reason why it is proper to admire anything must be constituted by the qualities which make the object of admiration

---

[8] At least in my second sense of "ought."

good, but it does not follow that the thought that it is good must, if the admiration is to be justifiable, intervene between the perception of the factual qualities admired and the feeling of admiration. Again it is clear that we cannot properly admire anything which is not good in that respect for which we admire it; but this would obviously be true on my definition also, indeed it would be a tautology. And we can certainly distinguish between our attitude of mind when we admire something spontaneously because its qualities directly call forth this emotion and our attitude when we admire it because we have first come to the conclusion that it ought to be admired, for example if I am at first prejudiced against somebody but realise that he is displaying qualities which I should greatly admire in somebody against whom I was not prejudiced. Of the two kinds of admiration the latter, so far from being preferable, is a feeble substitute for the former, unless and until it merges itself in the former. On the other hand, once the question of fittingness is raised at all, it is not easy for the emotion of admiration to attain much strength if we do not think that it is also fitting to feel it. But this is not to say that we need think its object good in a sense of "good" other than that in which the word expresses fitness to be admired. The emotion of admiration is different from the judgement that its object is one which it is fitting to admire, though the two are very closely connected.

(2) Ross, in view of (1), cannot say in general that to call something "good" means just that it is a fitting object of a pro attitude, though he does admit that in one of its primary senses "good" does stand for "fit object of satisfaction." [9] But in the other, as we have just seen, "good" is for him indefinable. He admits that, when we call something "good," we are always expressing a pro attitude towards it,[10] but he distinguishes

---

[9] Id., p. 279.
[10] Id., p. 254-5.

what is expressed from what is meant. The former must from the nature of the case be a psychological attitude of the speaker, but this need not apply to the latter. I should make the same distinction between expressing and meaning, and agree that, while ethical statements, like any others, *expressed* a state of mind of the speaker, they might *mean* something quite different. Even on my view "this ought to be admired" is different from "I feel admiration for this." The distinction is quite compatible with the view that what an ethical statement means is always that it is fitting to have some pro attitude.

(3) Ross prefers to define "good" in the sense other than "admirable" in terms of satisfaction rather than in terms of pursuit or choice.[11] No doubt whatever is a fit object of choice or pursuit for its own sake is a fit object of satisfaction, but serious difficulties arise when we consider degrees of goodness. It seems to me far from evident that it is fitting always to feel satisfaction in something in proportion to its goodness. It is by no means unfitting to feel more satisfaction in the happiness of my mother than in that of a total stranger, yet the two are equally valuable (at least if the stranger is equally deserving).[12] This is true even in cases where it is my duty to pursue the good of the stranger at the time rather than that of my mother.

(4) I have rather in mind the sense of "ought" or "right" in which these words express fittingness, Ross rather the specifically moral sense, though I do not see how his view could be worked out if we excluded the former sense. For instance, if we say that morally good acts are admirable, we must mean that it is fitting to admire them, not that we morally ought to admire them, unless we think that it is a moral duty to have (and not merely to cultivate) certain feelings, a view

---

[11] Id., p. 279.
[12] For the difficulties that such considerations present to my own theory, which seem to me not insuperable, v. below, pp. 192-93.

which Ross at any rate rejects on the ground that we cannot instantaneously alter our feelings and that "ought" implies "can."

(5) This difference is relevant to the difference between Ross and me on the next point, that which relates to one's own pleasure. Ross holds that one's own pleasure is never a good in the sense in which another person's is, or indeed in any strict sense of the word, because it is not our moral duty to pursue our own pleasure while it is our moral duty to pursue the pleasure of others. But, in the sense in which I have used "ought" here, is it not obvious that we ought to pursue our own pleasure? Other things being equal, it is plainly much more reasonable, fitting, appropriate that I should try to do what will increase my pleasure rather than what will diminish it. And we do in fact find that the word "ought" is constantly being used in cases where the only reason in mind for doing something is that it would give the person who did it pleasure or spare him pain.

It is a second question whether we can go further and say that we are under a moral obligation to do what is conducive to our own pleasure. The question is complicated by the fact that, other things being equal, the happier I am the more likely am I to do good to others. It might even be said, as it was by Kant, that it is our duty to do what increases our own happiness, but only because, if I do it, I am more likely to fulfil my other duties. It is certainly difficult to find a case in which an action is relevant solely to my own pleasure and to nobody else's, if only because the happier I am the more pleasant *ceteris paribus* I am likely to be as a companion to others. But there are many cases where something is likely to add to our own pleasure very materially but only minutely and imperceptibly to the pleasure of others. In such cases we should certainly not be inclined to use the term "duty" or "moral obligation" at all. This, I think, is partly because such cases are usually very trivial, and we rightly do not use the solemn word "duty" on trifling occasions, and partly because we have a strong natural inclination to seek our own pleasure even to excess. It is thought unlikely that we shall fail to seek it where we ought except through mistakes of judgement, which are not in themselves moral faults, or through passions the yielding to which is already wrong on other grounds. But if I ask whether it would be my duty to be as cheerful as I could, even if it made no difference whatever to anybody else's happiness or to the fulfilment of any other duties whether I was cheerful or not, I must answer that it would. Apart from such temptations as gluttony or passions like anger which injure others as well as oneself and indulgence in which, at least beyond a very limited degree, is intrinsically evil, why do people neglect to do what will be conducive to their own pleasure? If they do so, as often, through a genuine mistake of judgement, we must not say that they are morally to blame, but neither can we say so if they fail to further the pleasure of others as much as they might through an honest error of judgement. But I might know or believe that some action was conducive to my own pleasure and that there was no moral objection to it, and yet I might not do it. Why not? I do not see how this could occur except through a desire for something else which, though less productive of pleasure for me, was more immediately obtainable or otherwise attractive, or through laziness. The two cases may indeed both be brought under the former heading, since laziness is due to a desire to avoid present trouble. Now it does seem to me that it must be in some slight degree morally wrong to let oneself be swayed against reason by a present desire. Knowingly to act against reason must be in some degree morally blameworthy, even if what reason tells us is only that such and such a course will be most conducive to our own pleasure. But, as I have said, blameworthiness is usually slight in cases where only our own pleasure is at stake, and therefore we are apt not to apply the term "duty" in such cases, reserving it for more serious matters and thinking that, since most people already seek their own pleasure much too much, it is better not to encourage them in this by saying that it is a duty to seek it. However we do blame people morally if they eat to excess of kinds of food which they know are liable to give them severe indigestion or are grossly extravagant or give way excessively to moods of depression, and it would be far-fetched to explain this entirely by the effect either on other people or their own character. Part of the reason why such conduct is blameworthy is the direct one that it involves wantonly sacrificing one's own happiness through slackness or from a devotion to trivial goods. We should add, as Ross himself did at a time when he still believed it to be a *prima facie* duty to produce pleasure for oneself, that "it is only if we think of our own pleasure not as simply our own pleasure, but as an objective good, something that an impartial spectator would approve, that we can think of the getting it as a duty; and we do not habitually think of it in this way." [18] No doubt to think too much of one's own pleasure is both wrong and likely to defeat its own object, but on the other hand there is no doubt a vast loss of pleasure through people neglecting to take desirable precautions or making the efforts needed to secure it.

If I had not decided that it was a duty *ceteris paribus* to further one's own pleasure, I should have been forced to deny either that my own pleasure is a good or that it is a moral duty to pursue the good as far as we can. To my mind this is a strong argument for my conclusion about pleasure, since I have a strong inclination to think both these propositions self-evidently true. But, even if we decide that we have no moral

---

[18] Ross, *The Right and the Good*, p. 26.

obligation to pursue our own pleasure, we surely cannot deny that it is fitting (in my sense) to pursue it and unfitting to neglect it, so that it will still remain a good. We shall then escape dilemmas like that of Ross who has to hold that the same thing, namely a pleasant experience, is good from the point of view of a man who has not the experience but not good from the point of view of a man who has. I admit that his view is the logical consequence of his definition of "good," in the sense with which we are concerned here, as a morally suitable object of satisfaction, since there is a moral suitability about feeling sympathetic satisfaction in the happiness of others which does not arise in our own case.[14] But this seems to be an objection to his definition, since it makes the same thing both good and indifferent and forces him to contradict the proposition that my own pleasure is good, which seems to me an obvious truism.

The case of vicious pleasures may be cited against me. I should reply that we must distinguish their pleasantness from the characteristics which make them vicious. If it be objected that on my view we should at least be under a *prima facie* duty to pursue them because they are pleasant, I should reply that the objection is innocuous if we realise what is the only sense in which this would follow. It would only follow if it means that, provided we could obtain the same amount of pleasure in ways which were not immoral, we ought *ceteris paribus* to take action to obtain it, or that the fact that they have the universal characteristic of pleasantness (as opposed to being pleasant in the particular, evil way in which they are pleasant) is, as far as it goes, a reason why we ought to pursue them, though it is completely outweighed by others. This is, I think, quite compatible with the particular kind of pleasure felt being so bound up with the character of the experience as

---

[14] V. *Foundations of Ethics*, p. 281.

a whole that, the greater the pleasure, the worse the state of mind of, for example, one who enjoys cruelty.

It is certainly not true that, when we speak of a moral action as "good," we are never using "good" to mean "fitting object of choice"; but in the majority of cases I think it is impossible to distinguish "intrinsically good" as thus applied from "morally admirable." For "fitting object of choice" as applied to actions one would rather say "right." I also think that, when we speak of a man's character or life as good, we usually mean "worthy of moral admiration or approval"; though we should grant that it can also be good in the sense of being the kind of character or kind of life which it would be fitting to choose to have. A good character or a morally good life is assuredly a fitting object of pursuit, and is so not merely on account of any hedonistic advantages it may have for oneself or for others. But I do not believe that we are usually thinking of this when we appraise a character or life as good, and still less so when we thus appraise particular actions. We are rather thinking of their admirableness; and, as I have said earlier, there are cases of actions that we rightly admire which certainly ought not to be done for their own sake but only for their consequences. Certain aesthetic and intellectual activities will be, like many moral dispositions and actions, good in both senses, that is, fitting objects in themselves both of choice or pursuit and of admiration, though not in this case of moral admiration. In fact, I think everything that is good in the sense of being admirable will be good in the other sense, except some (not all) moral actions. The exception is made because some moral actions ought to be done only for their consequences and not for their own sake.

While I recognise that aesthetic and intellectual, as well as moral, activities are good in the sense of being fitting objects of admiration, I admit that there is an easily recognisable psychological difference between the kind of admiration that it is fitting to feel towards such objects and the kind that it is fitting to feel towards what is morally good. It has been contended, for example, by Hume, that the feelings with which we contemplate different kinds of moral virtue also differ, and this may well be the case. It certainly is so with the opposite emotions towards different kinds of morally evil actions. For instance, the kind of feeling with which it is appropriate to regard cheating is clearly different from the kind with which it is appropriate to regard cruelty, and this is not merely a difference in the degree but in the felt quality of the emotion. But we need not let these differences lead us, as they did Hume, to slur over or even repudiate the distinction between moral and other approval. For at any rate our feelings towards the display of different moral virtues have, despite their minor differences, something in common which they do not share with the feelings of admiration we have towards intellectual and aesthetic productions, though the latter feelings still belong to the same genus, admiration. The same applies even more clearly to the feelings of disapproval we have towards the display of different vices as compared with those we have towards the display of intellectual and aesthetic deficiencies.

It is irrelevant to object to my account on the ground that we cannot alter our emotions at a moment's notice and therefore cannot be told that we ought to feel a certain emotion but only that we ought to cultivate it. Perhaps "ought" in the sense in which it asserts moral obligation is applicable only where what it is said we ought to do could be brought about by an act of will on our part at the time; but we can certainly speak of the emotions a man "ought" to have in the sense of "the suitable emotions for him to have." It remains a fact that they are the suitable emotions whether he can feel them or not. We should use his inability for feeling them as a ground for denying that he ought to feel them in this sense of "ought" only if we held that he was by his constitution unalterably cut off from any emotions of that kind, as an animal is cut off from delight in philosophy.

The proposed definition of "good" as "fitting object of a pro attitude" can be applied to others of the senses of this word. If my definition is right, it will in fact explain why the word is used in so many different senses. For the sense will vary according to the particular pro attitude or attitudes the fittingness of which we intend to assert. This is to my mind both an argument for the definition and a reply to the naturalist who wants to know how it is that a word which in one sense stands for a simple indefinable quality should stand for something so different in other contexts. "Good" may, as I have pointed out earlier,[15] mean (1) pleasant or liked, (2) capable of satisfying desire, (3) efficient, (4) productive of something intrinsically good, (5) efficiently produced, (6) intrinsically good, (7) ultimately good, (8) as applied to characteristics, good-making, (9) morally good as applied to actions, (10) morally good as applied to persons. I have defined sense (6) as signifying what is a fitting object of welcome, choice, or pursuit for its own sake, and sense (7) can be defined in terms of sense (6), or vice versa if this is preferred. Sense (8) is obviously definable in terms of other senses, since "good-making" presupposes "good." Sense (9) I have defined as usually signifying "object of moral admiration," though it may also be used to mean "object of moral choice." Sense (10) seems also usually to mean "morally admirable," but here as applied to a person. Senses (2), (3), (4), and (5) signify that the object called "good" is a fitting object of approval or admiration in certain non-moral respects, or of choice if one desires to attain certain ends. (1) asserts rather that what is pronounced good is actually an object of a pro attitude than that it ought to be one; but we need not be

---

[15] V. above, pp. 112 ff.

surprised if common usage, which cannot be expected to make subtle distinctions, sometimes employs to signify "actual object of a pro attitude" a word which usually means "fitting object of such." The two senses are in such cases very closely connected because, if I regard something as capable of satisfying desire, I *ipso facto* regard it as in so far and subject to certain assumptions a fitting object of pursuit, though it may be open to objection in other respects so that it is on the whole not desirable to pursue it. With similar reservations, what is pleasant is regarded as a fitting object of liking. For a person with my sense of taste it is after all appropriate to like strawberries. So even where "good" means the object of an *actual* pro attitude, it stands for what is also at the same time regarded as a *fitting* object of such.

There are no doubt many different shades of meaning attached to the word "good" which neither I nor anybody else has distinguished in our classifications, but a place is left for these in my definition, though not in any narrower one. For in thinking of the good as a fitting object of a pro attitude we may sometimes have more in mind one of the numerous pro attitudes, sometimes another. We may sometimes think of it rather as a fitting object of desire, sometimes rather as a fitting object of satisfaction or choice or pursuit or approval, etc., thus giving scope for a great variety of minor differences of meaning within the definition that I have provided. In view of the vagueness of ordinary usage I cannot help regarding this as a point in favour of my definition.

I have defined one of the ethical concepts often taken as ultimate, namely good, in terms of another, fittingness. My definition of "good" also enables me to analyse another ethical notion which would otherwise have had to be taken as indefinable, namely, the notion of badness, and this I regard as one advantage of my view. The fewer unanalysed ethical concepts we have the better, provided we do not explain away facts. Now, if "good" is taken as unanalysable, "bad" will also have to be so taken, for it certainly is a positive notion and not merely equivalent to "not good." But if we analyse good as "fitting object of a pro attitude," it will be easy enough to analyse bad as "fitting object of an anti attitude," this term covering dislike, disapproval, avoidance, etc. The more specific meaning of the term will vary according to which of the different possible anti attitudes we have in view. To say that a man is bad is certainly not to say that we ought to take all the possible anti attitudes against him, including, for example, hate, but only the specific one of moral disapproval.

But there still remain two undefined concepts in ethics, though they are both expressed by the same word, "ought," namely (1) fittingness, (2) moral obligation.[16] Could we analyse either in terms of the other? I do not see how we could analyse fittingness in terms of moral obligation. Indeed I think that any such attempt would involve a vicious circle, for it is only because we first think an act fitting that we are under a moral obligation to perform it. There remains a possible way of defining "moral obligation" in terms of fittingness together with some psychological concept or concepts, as I defined "good." We might say that "A morally ought to do this" means (1) it would be fitting for A to do this, and (2) if he does not do it, it is fitting that he should be in that respect an object of the emotion of moral disapproval, or perhaps simply (2) without (1). This too sounds like a vicious circle, but it is not really one if we mean by "moral disapproval" either some specific emotion indefinable but introspectively recognisable and distinguishable from other kinds of disapproval, or else just disapproval felt for a person in respect of a certain kind of qualities of the will as distinct from, for example, qualities of the intellect or qualities of the

---

16 V. above, pp. 130 ff.

body. "To be a fitting object of disapproval" is equivalent to "deserving blame," "blame" being the expression of disapproval. I think it preferable to define moral obligation in this way rather than in terms of moral admiration. For there are many morally obligatory actions which we should not admire a man for performing, though we should blame him for not performing them. I do not deserve moral admiration because I pay my ordinary debts since I have no real temptation not to pay them, but I should certainly deserve moral disapproval if I failed to pay them. One might say that I deserve at any rate approval for paying them and then define moral obligatoriness in terms of moral approval, but the appropriate approval in these cases would be so tepid, since the merit incurred by me is so slight, as to make it unsuitable to use this in defining a concept so connected with marked emotions as is that of moral obligation. Further, the consciousness of obligation seems to be more closely connected with the notions of shame and disapproval as fitting "sanctions" if we do not do what we ought than with the notion of approval if we do. Good is more connected with the positive side, obligation with the negative side, of ethics.

This definition has the advantage of providing the minimum non-naturalist theory of ethics, by which I mean the non-naturalist theory which a converted naturalist could accept with least divergence from his previous views. For it admits only one unanalysable concept, and it is more difficult to deny that there is a relation of fittingness not analysable in purely psychological terms than to deny that there is a quality, goodness, which is not thus analysable. In these days when naturalist tendencies are so strong, it is more than ever worth while for a non-naturalist to ask "What is the maximum of concessions I can make to the naturalist without destroying my whole view of ethics," and for a naturalist to ask "Have I refuted all forms of non-naturalist ethics or only some?"

There still remains a radical difference between doing something because I think that I shall be an actual object of disapproval if I do not do it and doing it because I think I shall be a fitting object of disapproval (*deserve* blame). The view suggested would not, however, necessarily imply that even the latter is the usual motive of moral action. The main motive should normally be derived directly from an apprehension of the nature of the proposed act and its consequences, and so of its objective fittingness, not from the hypothetical fact that I should deserve blame if I acted differently. It is obvious that the latter consideration does often play a part, but it is better for a man to tell the truth because he hates lies than because he would deserve to be blamed if he told lies.

It may be doubted, however, whether the analysis given brings out the full specific nature of the ethical ought. If not, we may have to admit a second indefinable concept in ethics, moral obligation, as distinct from fittingness. There is another possibility. It is arguable that the concept of fittingness is all we can have in an ethics without a theology, and that anything additional in the content of moral concepts is really supplied by the notion of a personal God, or at any rate by the idea of sin as going against the fundamental nature of reality so that we are fighting against the main stream of the universe when we act wrongly. If this further concept is a necessary part of our ethical thinking, we shall then have an argument from ethics to the existence of God or to other metaphysical conclusions.

What is in a person's mind when he recognises something to be his moral duty? There is (a) the consciousness that it is fitting for him to do it; (b) the consciousness that, if he does not do it, he will deserve condemnation; (c) the concept that there is in some sense a law binding him to do it, which law, while it does not compel in the sense of taking away his liberty to disobey it, yet has authority in another meaning of the term, so that morality consists in acting as if he were compelled by it. It may be that the third element is a theological concept, or one which, if adequately analysed, would have to be developed into such. Is it clear that there is anything more in the concept of duty besides these three concepts? I doubt it.

Among the things to which the relational property of being fitting can belong are of course included actions, and one of the meanings of "rightness" as applied to an action is "fittingness in relation to the situation." If by this is understood fittingness in relation to the situation as a whole you have my first sense of "rightness," if fittingness in relation to the situation as apparent to reasonable human beings my third, if fittingness in relation to the situation as apparent to the agent my second sense of rightness (except in so far as this sense of rightness includes in addition the notion of moral obligation). To say that an action is right is not the same as to say that it is good, for to call it "good" would mean that not necessarily it but some pro attitude relative to it was fitting; but no doubt all right actions are good in some sense, for in relation to them some pro attitude is fitting, if only the pro attitude of doing them, and we do say that it is always good to do what is right. On the other hand a right action is not necessarily good if by "good" is meant "fitting object of admiration," hence the distinction made by many philosophers. It was right of me to pay my bus fare home, but I do not deserve to be admired for it. Nor, as I have pointed out, are all fitting actions actions which we ought to do in the sense of being morally obliged to do them. Sometimes the fitting action is one which we cannot do or do not think of doing, and then we are not morally obliged to do it. In such cases we may or may not be morally to blame for previous action or neglect to act which prevented us from being able to do it or think of doing it.

To return from the analysis of obligation to that of good,

I think that one of the chief reasons why my analysis is liable to appear unsatisfactory is simply due to a misunderstanding. It will be objected against me that it is only fitting to approve, or have a pro attitude towards, what is good because we first know or believe it to be good and that, if we did not believe it to be good, there would be no ground for such an attitude, so that the attitude would not be fitting. The answer is that the ground lies not in some other ethical concept, goodness, but in the concrete, factual characteristics of what we pronounce good. Certain characteristics are such that the fitting response to what possesses them is a pro attitude, and that is all there is to it. We shall not be any better off if we interpolate an indefinable characteristic of goodness besides, for it is no easier to see that it follows directly from the nature of things that they are good than it is to see that it follows directly from their nature that they are fitting objects of a pro attitude. We see directly that pleasant experiences as such, natural beauty, unselfish love, are fitting objects of pro attitudes. That they are follows necessarily from their specific nature, as Moore held that it followed that they had the simple property of goodness. If we ask why we should admire so-and-so the answer is to recite his good deeds, not just specify that he is good without explaining further how he is good.

In the case of moral, and perhaps in some other cases, of goodness the situation is, however, a little more complicated than these remarks would suggest. For the fittingness of adopting an attitude of moral admiration toward an action depends on the rightness of the action (that is, its fittingness in certain respects), that is, on another non-naturalist value fact, itself in turn dependent on the natural, factual characteristics of the action. This may be so also in the case of the goodness of an aesthetic experience. That may depend, not merely on the factual characteristics of its object, but on a certain quality which would have to be likewise understood in terms of a non-naturalist fittingness. In a great work of art the different parts fit together harmoniously and they are a fitting representation of reality, or at least human life, not in the copying sense but in some deeper sense, and these may be regarded as non-natural characteristics which condition the work being aesthetically admirable, as rightness in some sense is a necessary condition of an action being morally admirable. It is difficult to see how a merely naturalist analysis could do justice to aesthetic fittingness. And that would explain the inclination to say that a work of art is admirable only because it is first good in some other sense, though "right" or "harmonious" would perhaps be a better word. Again it may be said that knowledge is a fitting object of pursuit or approval only because it has the non-natural characteristic of being true. I should not, however, call this a value fact or value property. Knowing what is true may be valuable, but not truth itself as a property of propositions.

We may now explain how it is that the connection between "good" and "ought" seems synthetic and not analytic. We often think of "ought" as expressing not only fittingness but moral obligation; and to say that we are under a moral obligation, where we can, to produce what it is fitting to choose for its own sake is a synthetic proposition. It will moreover remain so even if "we morally ought" has to be analysed as equivalent to "we should be fitting objects of moral disapproval if we did not do so." Propositions as to what kinds of things it is fitting to approve or disapprove are obviously synthetic. In this case, however, the character of the transaction is liable to be concealed by the use of the same word, "ought," in two different senses. At the same time the fact that fittingness carries with it a moral obligation, where we can do what is fitting, explains why the same word, "ought," is used to cover both concepts.

Moore now thinks there is equally good reason for rejecting

the view that "intrinsically good" is definable in terms of "ought" and for rejecting the view that "ought" is definable in terms of "intrinsically good," [17] the reason being in each case that we can think of the *definiendum* without thinking of the alleged *definiens;* [18] and Rashdall maintains that it is quite consistent to hold both that "good" is indefinable in Moore's sense and that "we can only bring out the real meaning of the idea by the use of words which equally imply the notion of 'ought.' " [19] So it may be questioned whether I should not, instead of defining "good" in the way in which I did, have just admitted that "good" and "ought" are correlative and left it at that. Or it may be asked why I defined "good" in terms of "ought" when I might equally well have defined "ought" in terms of "good" by saying that "I ought to do A" meant "of the actions that were in my power at the moment A was that one which would be most effective as a means for the production of good." Now if, as seems to be the case, Rashdall and Moore were thinking of "ought" as including moral obligation in its meaning, I should contend that "good" is not definable in terms of "ought" thus understood; but it does not follow that it is not definable in terms of "ought" understood only as asserting fittingness. I defined "good" in terms of "ought" rather than "ought" in terms of "good," because I found that I could not form a clear concept of intrinsic goodness without including in it the concept of ought, but that I could form a clear concept of ought without including in it the concept of good. Ought is also a wider concept in extension, for there are mental attitudes which we can describe as fitting and which are yet not directed towards the good. There are also fitting mental attitudes possible

---

[17] *The Philosophy of G. E. Moore* (Library of Living Philosophers), p. 610.

[18] Id., p. 599.

[19] *Theory of Good and Evil*, Vol. 1, pp. 135–6 n.

towards evil things, the anti attitudes, and even a fitting attitude towards indifferent things, the attitude of ignoring them.

It has been said that, if there is nothing intrinsically good, only an "ought," this takes the value out of life. Clearly, if my view did "take the value out of life," the view would be false, because it purports to be an analysis of what is meant by saying that people find value in life. But the objection in question is due to forgetting that we are only analysing what is meant by goodness and not giving an account of what things are good. A statement of the abstract distinguishing feature which belongs to all good things or our relations to these must from the nature of the case be jejune and colourless, because it has abstracted from all the concrete content which belongs to such things. If we admitted an indefinable intrinsic goodness besides the "ought," this intrinsic goodness would still not be itself valuable. What would be of value would be the experiences which had it; and these will be of value in any case. The intrinsic goodness of an experience, whether definable or indefinable, is not an additional value which we enjoy; to appreciate the experience is to appreciate its goodness. Life is of intrinsic value in so far as it consists of experiences which are worth having for their own sake and comprises qualities which are worth admiring for their own sake: you cannot ask for more value than that. And the value of these experiences and qualities cannot possibly be diminished by coming to the conclusion that what is meant by saying they have value is that it is fitting to have a favourable attitude towards them. They will be just as good as before.

It has been objected that my view is excessively indirect on the ground that it involves saying that, when we judge something to be good, we are really judging not it but our attitude towards it. But we must remember that fittingness as a relation has two terms, so that to judge what attitude is fitting to A is at the same time to judge A. The judgement is

no more about ourselves, who constitute one term of the relation, than it is about A. To say it is fitting to approve A is to
say that A is of such a nature as to call for our approval. We
can only see whether we ought to have a pro attitude towards
something by seeing what the nature of that something is, and
the right pro attitude is dictated by its nature. We do not
first learn what attitudes towards A are fitting and then decide
that A is good; on the contrary to learn that certain attitudes
towards A are fitting is to learn that A is good.

It has also been objected that my view involves a vicious
infinite regress on the ground that, if to judge something good
is to judge that it is fitting to approve it, this amounts to saying
that to judge it good is to approve my approval and so on *ad
infinitum*. But the infinite regress would arise only if we
meant by "fitting" just "good" and therefore were defining
"good" in terms of itself. In that case to judge A good would
be to judge that it was good to approve A, and therefore it
would be to judge that it was good to approve of approving
A and so on *ad infinitum*. But, because "good" and "fitting"
are different terms, the regress need not be carried beyond its
second step. I did not say that "it is fitting to approve A"
meant "it is fitting to approve my approval of A," but only
that "A is good" meant "it is fitting to approve A." "Fitting"
must not be itself defined in terms of another fittingness or
of anything else whatever. "It is fitting to approve," I suppose,
entails "it is fitting to approve of approving A," and so on *ad
infinitum*; but it is no objection to the truth of a proposition
that it would entail the truth of an infinite number of propositions, unless it entailed that we could not assert the first
proposition intelligently without having already grasped all
these infinite other propositions. It is no objection to our
knowing the truth of the proposition that "London is the
capital of England" to say that it entails that it is true that it
is true that London is the capital of England and so on *ad*

infinitum. It would be an objection only if it were the case that we could not be justified in asserting that London was the capital of England without having first recognised the truth of this infinite number of propositions.

It has also been made an objection against my view that it makes all value judgements ultimately hypothetical. To say that "A is a fitting object of a certain pro attitude" would seem to mean either that, if any one adopts the attitude, he will be doing what is fitting, or that if any one is confronted with or thinks of A he ought to adopt the attitude. To this I should reply: (1) We have to admit in any case that the very important class of ethical judgements which assert that an action ought to be done are hypothetical unless and until the action to which they refer has been done.[20] If I ask what I ought to do next I am asking which of the alternative actions possible will have the attribute of fulfilling my obligations if it is done. It would not therefore be so paradoxical if we had to admit that judgements involving good are also hypothetical. (2) If there is nobody to have an attitude of approval towards them, "good" may still be viewed as a positive characteristic in whatever is good, namely, that of requiring approval. (3) In an actual case when I say "A is good," I am feeling approval of A myself, and therefore A is always the object of an actually existing pro attitude of a kind deemed fitting by me. True, my judgement does not confine itself to asserting that my attitude to A is fitting, but lays it down also that the attitude would be the fitting one for anybody else to have whether anybody is actually having it or not, so it may be contended that it is still partly hypothetical. But at any rate it has a categorical core, and this will explain why we are inclined to think all such propositions categorical not hypothetical in character.

---

[20] This is not to say that they are all hypothetical imperatives in Kant's sense, for their obligatoriness still does not depend merely on our desires.

A view like mine is for various reasons in a particularly strong position as against naturalism. In the first place, naturalism is commonly supported by doubts as to whether we can really be aware of an indefinable quality, goodness, but it is impossible to doubt at any rate that we are aware of some relation signified by the term "ought" and *prima facie* different from any purely psychological relation. As long as the only alternative to some form of naturalism or subjectivism seems to be the view that good is just a simple quality, it seems open to doubt whether naturalism or subjectivism is not true. It has been asked whether anybody besides a few philosophers has thought they could perceive such a simple quality. But it cannot be doubted that practically everybody is aware of the relations of fittingness and moral obligation, which are lumped together under the term "ought," though they may not always distinguish them clearly. The difficulty arose, on my view, through looking for the indefinable where it could not be found. We are not clearly aware of an indefinable non-natural goodness, but we are of fittingness and obligation. Now on my view the reason why a naturalist definition of "good" is unsatisfactory is, not because good is indefinable, but because these relations are included in the notion of good. A principal objection made by me against naturalist definitions of "good" was just that, if "good" were defined naturalistically, it would be no more rational, right, fitting to pursue the good than the bad and that good would carry with it no moral obligation to pursue the good.

Secondly, the most popular naturalist modes of analysis of good are in terms of various pro attitudes, such as interest or approval. Now I have defined "good" as what ought to be the object of a pro attitude. So, if the view I have suggested is true, what the naturalists are doing is to take the concrete, more distinctly perceptible element in goodness but omit the relational element. Therefore, although people feel as if some-

thing had been left out, they, misled partly by the fact that
"good" is grammatically an adjective, look for some other
quality and, being unable to find it, become more and more
inclined to adopt a naturalist view. My theory explains the
connection between emotional attitudes and judgements
about goodness or badness, which connection is often taken
as an argument for naturalism. In general, if a judgement
about the goodness of something is simply a judgement to the
effect that we ought to have a certain attitude, we can easily
see how it is that people have taken it to be a judgement about
the attitude actually adopted. The only other element in my
analysis besides the purely psychological ones is a relation,
and it is a well known historical fact that philosophers have
been apt to overlook the importance of relations. We are not
conscious of relations with the same vividness and distinctness
as we are of qualities, and they are harder to abstract from the
rest of our experience and thought. We do not have a distinct idea of what it is like to perceive between-ness or with-
ness, in the sense in which we have a distinct idea of what it is
like to see blue or to feel fear. And what I have said applies
most of all to formal, very general relations like the one in
question. Even the vitally important relation of logically
necessary connection or entailment is hardly noticed as a
special relation by anybody but philosophers, though it must
be apprehended in particular instances by everybody who
can argue at all. It is no more difficult to admit the relation
of fittingness than to admit, the relations of similarity or consistency, or even the relations expressed by "of" or "towards"
in "approve of" or "feel emotions towards," relations which
even the naturalist must admit in his account of ethics. None
of these relations can really be said to be given in sensation.

So we can see how those already disposed not to admit any
non-naturalist element in knowledge could persuade themselves that they had given an adequate analysis of ethical con-

cepts when, fastening on the only concrete non-relational elements in the concept, they had analysed good in terms of the same psychological factors that I admit in my analysis but had left out the relation or relations signified by "ought." I thus admit an important element of truth in naturalism. It is in any case difficult to believe that we could have formed the idea of good if we had never had any pro attitudes and this is used as an argument for naturalism. My view gives an explanation alternative to naturalism.

It is also easier to understand how the subjectivist theory that "good" is relative to the person judging could grow up, for "good" is relative to some person or other in the sense that it means that towards which it is fitting for a person to have a pro attitude. This being so, it is easy to fall into confusion and regard it as relative in some other sense. We may agree that it would be senseless to speak of anything as good if nobody could conceivably ever desire or appreciate it; but the view does not require that it should be actually desired or appreciated by anybody. It may well be the case that it is fitting to desire and appreciate something which men are not yet developed enough to desire or appreciate. I make good and evil relative to all rational beings, not only to human beings, and this in two respects: (1) If it is fitting for somebody to have a pro attitude towards a, the judgement that it is thus fitting for him will be true, whoever makes it, whether man, Martian, angel, or God. (2) If it is fitting for any being to have a pro attitude towards a as such in a given respect, it will be fitting for any other being who knows what a is factually like also to have a pro attitude.[21] This will apply even if

---

[21] The pro attitude will, however, not necessarily always be the same. It may be fitting for A to admire B without its being fitting for B to admire himself. Or it may be fitting for A to be grateful to B, who has rendered him great services, without its being fitting for C to be grateful to B where C knows of B's services to A but has himself received no such benefits from B. But it will be fitting for everybody to adopt some pro attitude in all cases

a is only judged good as a means to something else, since the causal laws which make it a good means are not dependent on the subjective characteristics of the person who judges whether or not they hold, but it is more important to see that it is true of intrinsic goodness. This is not to say that all rational beings will be able to appreciate *a* in all cases where *a* is good; but if not they will not be able to take a fitting attitude towards *a*. A tone-deaf man cannot take a fitting attitude towards Beethoven's music as such, because he does not know what it is like, though he may of course take a fitting attitude towards the situation created by his own deficiencies. Usually the inability to appreciate *a* will occur because the person in question cannot obtain the experience requisite to find out what *a* is like factually, but it may be due to lack of the requisite emotional capacity. This is not of course the same as to say that all rational beings who know *a* ought morally to have a pro attitude towards *a*. If they do not have it, they are lacking in some respect, but they are not necessarily morally to blame for this.

Actions, it may be urged, present an exception to the rule I have laid down, since in the same objective situation a particular action may well be right for me and wrong for you. But the whole situation relevant to the rightness of the action includes subjective as well as objective factors; and, if these are taken into account, the action as done by me would not be the same as the action as done by you, and it would be quite consistent to approve of one action and disapprove of the other. If the action as done by me is really good it is fitting that all rational beings who know of it should feel approval, and unfitting that they should not; and this is true even

---

where the admiration or gratefulness of A is justified. B should not admire himself, but he should realise that to do what he was doing was in certain respects preferable to different courses, otherwise there would be little merit in his doing it, and, without being grateful to B, C should approve B's action *qua* beneficial to A.

where they are of such a nature that for them it would have been quite wrong to do what I did. Even a person of very ordinary intelligence is quite capable of making this distinction and approving of, for example, the marriage of A to B, while realising quite well that it would not have been at all appropriate for himself to marry B, even if it had been possible for him to do so. I think it is implied by the notion of goodness that anything which we rightly regard as intrinsically good will be a fitting object of a pro attitude on the part of any beings who know what it is like, though whether and how it can be attained will depend on conditions which are not necessarily the same for all rational beings but might vary widely as between us and, for example, the inhabitants, if any, of Mars or Venus. It is very difficult to see how we could ever be justified in saying something was good if no human being, even if he knew what it was, were capable of appreciating it; but some propositions are no doubt true which we could never be justified in asserting, and there is certainly no self-contradiction in the suggestion that there are such non-human goods. I think it is likely that there are; the universe is rich. It would be rash of a canine philosopher to say that nothing was good which could not be appreciated by a dog.

My analysis would also explain how it is that the application of "good" and "bad" are in the first instance learned through noticing and imitating the emotional attitudes of others. As these circumstances are often regarded as constituting a strong argument for naturalism, this may be of some importance. A young child seems to learn the application and even the meaning of the words "good" and "bad" by hearing them spoken in tones or with gestures that indicate approval or disapproval, and this is taken as evidence that "bad" *means* "disapproved," and that "good" means "approved." But clearly, if "bad" does not mean just "what is disapproved" (either by the speaker or by people generally) but "what ought to be disapproved," this will also explain why the expression of approval or disapproval is the natural and normal way of teaching a child both what is meant by "good" or "bad" and to what things he should apply the terms. For, in so far as "good" means that towards which you ought to feel approval and "bad" that towards which you ought to feel disapproval, it follows that in order to teach a child the meaning and application of the terms you must express to it the attitudes of approval and disapproval on suitable occasions. In so far as "good" means "what we ought to pursue" and "bad" "what we ought to avoid," ethical education will consist in inducing the child by example and precept to pursue and avoid what it is suitable to pursue or to avoid. If to call something "good" only signifies that it is a fitting object of certain attitudes, it is easy to see why the attitudes should figure predominantly in learning the use of the word. The attitudes are expressed by others as a means to inducing the child to take them himself. Now we learn best to do the right things by doing them ourselves, and therefore in order to learn when it is fitting to take certain attitudes the child must be encouraged to take them himself.

My definition also has the advantage over any other I know, whether naturalist or non-naturalist, of explaining how it is that "good" is used in so many different senses, a fact which has for many minds been a serious obstacle to taking the view that it ever stands for a simple indefinable quality intuitively perceived. On my view it naturally will stand for various different senses according to the pro attitude in question. Further, if goodness is, as I have suggested, a relational property, this makes it easier to maintain that it is a non-natural concept, for all other plausible cases of such concepts are, I think, cases not of qualities but of relational properties.

A criticism which some will direct against me is that I have already surrendered the fort, because the only non-natural concept retained by me in ethics is not one that is specifically ethical at all, but one that belongs even to purely prudential action. However even purely prudential action presupposes value judgements, if only that one's own pain is bad and one's own pleasure good. What is wrong with egoistic hedonism is not that it does not presuppose a goodness which if it is to serve the purpose even of the egoistic hedonist could not be equated with an empirical property, but that it is unduly limited in its view as to what things are good and what things we ought to pursue. It may, however, be argued that, while I admit value judgements, I do not do justice to those judgements which are specifically ethical. But it may be that the distinction between specifically ethical and other value judgements is not that the former admit new simple concepts not included in the latter but that they admit a new class of things as having value. I am not indeed prepared to commit myself to the view that there is no irreducible non-naturalistic value concept except fittingness, since I am not fully satisfied with the proposed analysis of moral obligation in terms of fittingness; but in any case fittingness, as understood by me, is not to be equated with the characteristic of being an effective means to the production of something. That fittingness is not to be thus identified is shown by the fact that it is often fitting to do something or aim at something for its own sake and not merely as a means. Further, even where we perform some act merely as a means to something else, its fittingness as a means could not be a ground why it was morally obligatory or even prudent to do it, unless it was also fitting to treat its results or some of them as ends-in-themselves. Nor, when I say that it is fitting to admire morally good actions, do I mean merely that our admiration is a useful means to something else. In none of these three cases could "fitting" possibly be translated as just "efficient as a means."

Why did I make fittingness rather than moral obligation the fundamental concept of ethics? Might I not have analysed the fittingness of doing A in terms of the moral obligation to do A if we could? My reasons for not adopting this course were as follows: (a) It is clear that for me to be under a moral obligation to do A I must first believe that it is fitting for me to do A. Therefore the concept of moral obligation presupposes the concept of fittingness and not vice versa. (b) There is no verbal contradiction in saying both that my own pleasure is a good and that I am never under a *moral* obligation to pursue it as such, or in saying that I am under no moral obligation to sacrifice somebody else's lesser good for the sake of my own greater good. Therefore we cannot use "ought" in the moral obligation sense when defining "good." (c) As we have seen, "good" does not always mean only what ought to be chosen; it sometimes means what ought to be admired, or be the object of other pro attitudes such as desire or liking, and we cannot say that we are under a moral obligation to admire, desire, or like something, but we can say that we ought, in the fittingness sense, to have these feelings towards it.

CHAPTER VI

Consequences of the Analysis for a General Theory of Ethics

What bearing has my analysis on the question of the general criteria for determining what is right? Here the chief controversy in recent years has perhaps been between the "ideal utilitarians," who make the right depend solely on the good, and the adherents of a view like that of Ross, who maintains that we have "*prima facie*" duties not explicable simply by reference to the amount of good produced or likely to be produced. The "ideal utilitarian," while not restricting good to pleasure as the hedonistic utilitarian does, insists that the ultimate ground which makes an action right must always be its conduciveness to the production of good. Others have maintained in opposition that there is no necessary connection between good and ought and that it may quite well be our duty, for example, to keep a promise even though there is every reason to think that we could do more good by breaking it. In this connection Sir David Ross introduced the conception of "*prima facie* duties," by which he means obligations which hold not absolutely but only in the absence of a stronger obligation.[1] To say we have a *prima facie* duty to do a certain kind of thing is thus to say that we ought to do it on its own account, *other things being equal.* To do what will produce the greatest good is held by him in this sense to be a *prima*

---

[1] Ross, *The Right and the Good,* Chap. II.

facie duty,[2] but not the only one. Thus we have also, for example, a *prima facie* duty to keep promises or to make reparation for wrongs we have done, that is, the fact that I have, for example, made a promise is always an *independent* reason why I should keep it; and if these obligations conflict with the obligation to produce the greatest good, they will not necessarily give way to it. They may do so or may not, but no general rule can be laid down for deciding which obligation should be regarded as more binding.

There is no doubt that Ross's view represents better than utilitarianism the way in which we actually think, but it still may be held that the latter gives a better account of the ultimate reason why acts are obligatory. Now I think we must admit with Ross that the obligation, for example, to keep promises, is not to be explained solely by the consequences of doing so; but the utilitarian, if he is not also a hedonist, may meet this by maintaining that the practice of keeping promises is good-in-itself, or at least that the action of breaking a promise is intrinsically bad. In that case the obligation would not be explained entirely by the consequences, actual or likely, of the act, and yet it would be derivable from the obligation to produce the greatest good, as the utilitarian maintains. For in the good produced by an action must be included not only the good lying in its consequences but also any intrinsic goodness that belongs to the action itself in its own right. This intrinsic good might indeed be outweighed by the badness of its consequences, so that the ideal utilitarian must admit the possibility of circumstances arising which would make it a duty to break a promise or violate other laws which are generally morally binding. But in this he would be in agreement with Ross, who holds that two *prima facie* duties may clash and that one will then have to give way to the other.

---

[2] With certain modifications of detail which we need not discuss here.

Now, if the utilitarian takes the line indicated, it seems impossible to refute his theory at the usual level at which the controversy is conducted. But suppose we define "good" as "what ought to be chosen, produced, or pursued." Then to say that something is "intrinsically good" will be to say that one ought to choose, produce, or pursue it on its own account, not indeed under all circumstances, because its production or pursuit might involve the sacrifice of something better, but at any rate other things being equal. But this is to say that we have a *prima facie* duty to choose, produce, or pursue it. So to give a list of our different *prima facie* duties will be to give a list of the different kinds of things (including actions) which are intrinsically good.[3] What would then be meant by "the greatest good"? Presumably that which we ought to pursue, produce, or choose above all other alternatives. This might seem to make utilitarianism a tautology, but it would at any rate be a Pyrrhic victory for the latter. The utilitarian principle is that what we ought to do is derivable from the good, while the reverse is true if my analysis is correct. The utilitarian would be guilty of a vicious circle if he insisted on deriving the "ought" from the "good" and then accepted an analysis which made "good" itself definable in terms of "ought." That it makes the principle that we ought always to produce the greatest good in our power necessarily true seems to me the chief argument for utilitarianism against Ross's view, for it is hard to believe that it could ever be a duty deliberately to produce less good when we could produce more; but, if the analysis I have given were adopted, this principle would be accepted in a form which did not contradict the contentions of Ross, for to say that we ought to produce the greatest good in our power would then only be to say that we ought to act

---

[3] I have pointed out that "intrinsically good" may be applied to actions both in this sense and in the different sense of "being fitting objects of admiration." I am not here talking about the latter sense.

in the way which was preferable above all others; that is, the way which ought to be chosen. The antithesis between a view which based the "ought" on the "good" and a view which based it on *prima facie* duties would thus disappear. There would disappear also the duality between two kinds of moral criteria, conduciveness to the production of good and fulfilment of obligations independent of the good produced, which must be present in any non-utilitarian view that does not disregard consequences altogether. This is surely in so far a gain. There would still be an antithesis between a view according to which what we ought to do depended entirely on consequences and a view according to which it depended partly on the intrinsic nature of the action; but the former view seems to me very unreasonable, for surely we must take account of the intrinsic nature of an action before we decide whether to do it or not. There would also be an antithesis between a view like that of the Hebrews which emphasized more the ought of moral obligation and a view like the Greek which emphasized more the ought of fittingness and the attractive nature of concrete ends. But the particular antithesis under discussion between Ross and the utilitarians would have gone.

Ross might indeed reply that he did not mean by a "*prima facie* duty" what one ought to do in the fittingness sense of "ought," which was the sense in which "ought" occurred in my definition of "good," but in the moral-obligation sense of "ought." But it is clear that for an action to be one which I ought to do in the latter sense it must also be one which I believe I ought to do in the former. It can hardly be my moral duty to do something which I do not believe to be the most fitting thing in the circumstances to do. Therefore of the two senses of "ought" the fittingness sense must be basic, in that I cannot determine what I ought to do in the other sense without first considering what I ought to do in the "fittingness" sense of "ought." This is so even if the moral-obligation sense is not analysable in terms of the fittingness sense, as I suggested it might possibly be. And therefore it is fittingness which we must consider in discussing the ultimate reasons which put us under a moral obligation to do some things rather than others. For it is not on the question whether we morally ought to do what is fitting that the utilitarians and Ross are at variance, but on the question what actions are fitting and why they are so. To the former question both sides would give an affirmative answer.

I distinguished earlier the sense of "good" in which it means "fitting object of choice or pursuit" from the sense in which it means "worthy of admiration," and if good was analysed in the latter way it would not carry with it the consequences I have suggested, for it is a synthetic proposition that it is always fitting to produce the state of affairs which is most worthy of admiration (and not, I think, a true one). But this cannot be the sense of "good" under discussion in the utilitarian controversy, since this dispute is about what we ought to do, and therefore we are in it directly concerned with fitting choices and not with fitting admiration or other emotional attitudes. Again, it is certain that pleasure is not "admirable" (worthy of admiration), and yet it is reasonable to say in the sense under discussion between Ross and the utilitarians that pleasure is good.

It may be objected that there seem clearly to be cases where it is at least arguable that the act which I ought to perform is not, as far as we can tell, the act which is likely to produce the greatest good, for example the case of stealing from a rich miser in order to give to a deserving poor man. It seems a perfectly intelligible and not self-contradictory position to admit both on the one hand that I should do more good if I stole the money and gave it to the poor man and on the other that I still ought to refrain from stealing it. But I suggest that the distinction here is really between (a) what I ought to prefer in abstraction from the only available means of producing it, (b) what I ought to choose to produce with the means at my disposal. Thus I ought to prefer in the abstract that A who is poor should have £100 rather than B who is rich, but I ought not to choose that he should have it through my stealing. We think it a greater good, that is a state of affairs which it is more fitting to produce, in itself, that A should have the hundred pounds, and other things being equal I ought to bring this about if I have the chance. But other things are not equal, since I can only bring it about by stealing, and it may still be better that B should have the hundred pounds, and not A, than that A should have the hundred pounds obtained by stealing.

A similar objection is that, if "the greatest good" means "that which we ought to choose in preference to any other," it would seem to follow that it was a tautology to say that I ought, apart from ulterior consequences, always to choose my own greater good in preference to somebody else's lesser good, or the greater good of a total stranger in preference to my mother's lesser good. But these statements are not tautologies. They would be hotly disputed, and to dispute them is certainly not equivalent to the self-contradiction of asserting that the greater good is not greater. Therefore it may be objected that my theory is mistaken since it makes into a tautology what is plainly a synthetic proposition. To this objection we may reply in the same way as we did to the previous one. What I am choosing in cases like this is not just my mother's good but my mother's good as produced by myself. (I cannot indeed, strictly speaking, choose the former in abstraction from the latter.) Now the production of my mother's good by myself is a different thing from the production of my mother's good by a stranger, and therefore it might easily be the case that I ought to choose the production of my mother's good by myself in preference to the production of a stranger's equal good by myself, and yet that the stranger's son ought to choose the production of his parent's good by himself in preference to the production of my parent's good by himself. To speak of the good of the parents as equal means that, other things being equal, neither has more claim to pursuit than the other; but, if I have a special relation involving obligation to one person which I have not to the other, other things are not equal. It does not follow, because the good of A and that of B are equally worth pursuit *per se,* that therefore the whole—good of A plus the pursuit and attainment of A's good by me—will have a value equal to the other whole—good of B plus the pursuit and attainment of B's good by me. Similarly, production of my own good by myself is lacking in a value possessed by the action of producing somebody else's good, or, to put it in other words, it is sometimes fitting to choose to produce another's good rather than my own, just because it is his, not mine. The reverse may also be true; it would not be right of me to sacrifice my own moral good by, for instance, dishonesty on the ground that if I did not take an opportunity of stealing somebody else would and that I was therefore unselfishly sacrificing my good in order to save his.

The objection would be stronger if I gave "ought to be desired" as an analysis of good. To say that I ought to desire the good of a stranger as much as the good of my mother is quite obviously false. Nor can my desire for the good of my mother be reduced to the desire that I should produce her good, for it is fitting that I should desire her good more than the equal good of a stranger even in cases where it is not in my power to produce it, or where for special reasons, for instance because I have made a promise, it is my duty to further the stranger's good rather than hers. The same applies to Ross's definition of "good" as "worthy or fit object of satisfaction," [4] since it is also fitting that her good should give me more satisfaction. If and when such an analysis of "good" gives the true meaning of the word, we must admit that what is good relatively to me is not always equally good relatively to you.[5] We could then call the goods of two different people equal only in relation to a third observer who had no special relations of affection or obligation to either of the parties. I think this a reason for defining "good" in most usages in terms of some pro attitude other than desire or satisfaction.

Were then the people who disputed as to whether the utilitarian principle was or was not true merely getting excited about a tautology? Surely there was a real issue? But we must remember that to say that, if certain propositions are analysed in a certain way, they become tautologies is not the same as to say that the proposition that they are to be analysed in that way is itself a tautology. Further, the controversy is certainly mixed up with questions which cannot be settled simply by accepting my analysis. There is in the first place the question whether the rightness (fittingness) of an action depends solely on its consequences, actual or likely. Of this question my analysis certainly does not dispose, for it is possible compatibly with this analysis either to include actions among the things which ought to be chosen on their own account or not. The question is not indeed identical with the question whether utilitarianism is true, for one might return a negative answer to it, while remaining a utilitarian, by including in the good produced a goodness belonging to the action itself as such. But it may be contended that utilitarians have not paid enough attention to this possibility, while non-utilitarians have not paid sufficient attention to the consequences.

Further, even if we grant that we ought always to choose

---

[4] *Foundations of Ethics,* pp. 275, 279.
[5] Ross makes this admission, id., p. 282.

the greatest good in the sense in which "ought" signifies "fittingness," it may still be contended that it does not follow that we are always under a moral obligation to choose the greatest good; and this might still be made an object of dispute, especially as Ross meant by *prima facie* duty not merely what is fitting but what is, other things being equal, morally obligatory. Most people would admit that their own pleasure was good and a fitting object of pursuit, but would deny that they were under a moral obligation to pursue it. I think it is clearly self-evident that we cannot be under a moral obligation to do anything unless we think this the most fitting course available, but the converse proposition that whatever course we think most fitting is morally obligatory on us is somewhat less certain (chiefly owing to the doubts about the obligatoriness of pursuing one's own pleasure), though I have a strong inclination to believe it true *a priori*.

The conception of *prima facie* duties has sometimes been criticised on the ground that it is clearly secondary and presupposes the conception of absolute rightness, and some justification for this criticism is provided by Ross's suggestion that they are to be viewed as *tendencies* to be absolute duties.[*] But to say that something is a *prima facie* duty is surely already to say not merely that there is a tendency for it to be fitting that we should adopt a certain attitude to it, but that it is absolutely fitting that we should do so, and also absolutely obligatory on us as far as it is in our power to take up the attitude at all. The attitude in question is not necessarily that of performing the act; this will be fitting only if certain other conditions are fulfilled. But it is categorically, not merely hypothetically, fitting that we should take the attitude of approving the proposed act in the respect under consideration (even if it would be wrong on the whole), of considering its

---

[*] *The Right and the Good*, pp. 28–9; *Foundations of Ethics*, p. 86.

performance favourably in this respect, of deploring and trying to make up for the omission if we cannot fulfil the *prima facie* duty without violating another more important, of mitigating our condemnation of the act in so far as it has this feature in its favour, etc. As a matter of fact, even in the exceptional cases where it is our duty, for example, to break a promise, we shall never, if we act rightly, let our attitude and hardly ever our behaviour be quite unaffected by the fact that we have promised. We shall, for instance, explain ourselves to the promisee and offer to make it up to him in some other way.[7] We shall at least regret the breach of faith. We shall look about for ways of avoiding it. We shall probably ask for release from the promise, if we can communicate with the promisee in time, rather than just break it. In general we shall adopt a pro attitude towards the act *qua* keeping a promise, though perhaps an anti attitude towards it in other respects, for instance, *qua* greatly hurting somebody. That we have made a promise must always be a factor to be taken into account, and to take anything into account is a positive attitude even if it does not lead to action in accord with the promise being taken, but it is hardly conceivable that the ideally right way of performing whatever action is performed would not be appreciably affected by the fact that we have promised. Still more obvious is it that, when we refer to a whole class of acts and describe promise-keeping as a *prima facie* duty, we are enjoining a very important positive attitude towards a large part of conduct. The primary ethical intuition, I think, is not that any action as a whole is fitting or unfitting, but that it is fitting or unfitting in certain respects. It is indeed often the case that we are entitled to conclude that an action

---

[7] The obligation to do this is most doubtful in cases where the promise has been extracted from us by violence or fraud, but in such cases it is doubtful whether there is even any *prima facie* fittingness about keeping it. If there is, it is certainly appropriate to regret breaking it.

is unfitting as a whole from having seen only its unfittingness in one particular respect, but this is because in such cases there is obviously no other aspect that we can see to counterbalance this or because the action seems to be done from a motive which would make the action immoral even if it happened by some accident to have good consequences, as when a man squanders on his own pleasures money without which it will be impossible for him to pay his debts.

Some of the difficulties in ethics no doubt arise because of the different senses in which "good" is used; that is, the different pro attitudes which people have in mind when they call something "good," or are at least aggravated by these differences. For instance, it is contended on the one hand that all goods must be commensurable because we have to decide between them in order to act, and on the other hand that it can never be morally right to sacrifice moral good for the sake of any other kind of good. In dealing with this question I should first ask in what sense "good" was being used. If we mean by "good" what ought to be admired, it is obvious that pleasure is not good and moral virtue is. If we mean by "good" what it is fitting to welcome or take satisfaction in, it seems to me that it would be unreasonable asceticism to insist that it is fitting to welcome less or take less satisfaction in the happiness of millions than in a slight moral advance by one man. If "good" means "desirable," it seems to me still clearer that it is fitting to desire the former more than the latter. If "good" means what ought to be pursued or chosen, the answer seems to me similar except for one reservation. Suppose I had to choose between causing a slight moral advance in myself or somebody else and giving a great deal of pleasure to millions and could not do both. Suppose in that case I believed it was my moral duty to do the latter. Then for that very reason I should be sacrificing moral good as well as pleasure if I did not do it, for I should then be doing the morally worse action.

There is then a sense in which it could never be my moral duty to sacrifice my present moral good for any amount of pleasure (or, for that matter, moral good) of anybody else. For suppose it were my duty to sacrifice it. In that case I should be doing my duty and therefore not sacrificing my present moral good, so the supposition is a self-contradictory one. But it might well be my duty to sacrifice some future moral good. For example it might be my duty for various reasons to accept a post although it seemed likely to me that the post would have in some degree bad effects on my character. A situation like this must very commonly arise. It is a well founded psychological generalization that a post carrying with it a great deal of money and power is more likely to be bad than good for the character of most people who have the chance of obtaining it, yet it is certainly often their duty to accept it and incur this risk for the sake of the good they may do.

Another difficulty for the ideal utilitarian, and indeed for other writers on ethics, is this. An infinite amount is obviously greater than any finite amount. Therefore it seems to follow that, however much higher in the scale of values virtue is than pleasure, provided the two are commensurable at all, any finite amount of virtue or higher good, however large, would be less good than an infinite amount of pleasure. In that case there would be more good in the life of a single being which enjoyed itself continually without achieving any other goods except pleasure, provided that being lived for ever, than there would be in the lives of any finite number of beings who lived for only a finite time, however much non-hedonistic good was realized in their lives, since that could not *ex hypothesi* be infinite. Yet surely if we had the power either to create a universe in which there existed only one being with a consciousness like that of a lower animal which lived for ever and enjoyed itself in its own way continually, or to create one in which there were a number of beings with finite lives possessed of goodness, happiness, love, knowledge, and aesthetic experience far beyond that of the best and most fortunate men we know, it would be fitting and our duty to create not the former but the latter? This may be used as an argument against utilitarianism, whether hedonistic or ideal; but a difficulty is left even if we discard utilitarianism, because it is almost or quite as paradoxical to say that the first universe would be a better universe than the second as it would be to say that we ought to create the first universe rather than the second. The difficulty seems to arise from taking too quantitative a view of good and to disappear if we realise that to call something good is not to say that it has a quality, goodness, of which you can have more or less, but to say that we ought to have certain attitudes towards it. If so, it ceases to seem evident that an infinite amount of certain good kinds of experience would be better than a finite amount of certain other good kinds. It does not by any means follow that, if we ought to produce something, other things being equal, we ought to produce an infinite amount of it in preference to a finite amount of any other kind of thing which we ought to produce. This seems to follow only if we assume that the sole reason for producing something is because it has a certain quality, goodness, distinct from the fact that we ought to produce it. In that case, since the only legitimate reason for action is constituted by this quality, goodness, the only reason for choosing A rather than B must be because A possesses or is likely to bring into existence a greater amount of this quality than B. But it need not be, on my view. Similarly, if goodness is a quality, A must have more of this quality than B if it is to be better than B; but, if to say that something is good is to say that we ought to take a pro attitude to it, it is again not evident that the strength of our pro attitude towards an infinite series ought to be greater than the strength of our pro attitude towards any finite series. We cannot in any case be expected to approve or welcome infinitely the infinite series.

My analysis thus removes what seems to me a serious difficulty for ethics, and I do not see how it can be removed as long as we hold that goodness is a quality possessed by all good things. Two other solutions have been suggested, but neither of them seems to be acceptable. One is to say that the goodness of pleasure and the higher kinds of goodness are incommensurable, so that no amount of pleasure, however great, can exceed in value any amount of moral goodness, however small. But this seems to me totally incredible. It surely would be less of an evil for me to do something slightly immoral, for example, not make as much effort as I morally ought to concentrate on my work during the next half-hour, than it would be for the whole human race to suffer intense agony or even to lose all pleasure for the space of a year, even if this made no difference for good or evil to their moral character? Another suggested solution is that, though pleasure is always in some degree good, so that the longer the hypothetical lower animal lived the better, the degree of goodness attached to a given amount of pleasure enjoyed by it might diminish progressively after a certain point, so that, when its existence had gone on for a very long time, the goodness of each successive increment of pleasure asymptotically approached zero.[8] But this also seems to me very difficult to hold, for I cannot see why the animal's pleasures should be supposed to diminish in value the longer it lived, provided their intensity as pleasures did not diminish. The animal could not be morally blamed for confining itself to the lower pleasures. We need not suppose it to be dissatisfied or bored with them; and, if it were, this would contradict the hypothesis by showing itself in a diminution of pleasure. No doubt the value of a total life may be

---

[8] V. McTaggart, *The Nature of Existence*, Vol. II, § 852.

viewed as dependent not only on the value of its parts but on the way in which these are related, and the value, if any, dependent on the relation of the successive stages of the animal's life might conceivably diminish to zero as its monotonous life continued. But this would not affect the value of its successive pleasant states of consciousness in themselves, which would surely be as great in the later as in the earlier ones, provided they were equally pleasant. It might still be argued that, however small the value of each specious present was, the total value of the infinite series would surpass any finite quantity of another good, whether or not it was augmented by any value due to the relation of its parts. The success of my theory in solving the difficulty where other objective theories fail is in my opinion an argument in its favour. This is not the only point in regard to which difficulty has been felt about a quantitative treatment of good. Yet the ordinary view is bound to treat good quantitatively, for choice between alternatives must depend on one alternative having more of this quality, goodness, than another in so far as the choice is dependent on the quality goodness at all, as it must in some cases be dependent, even on Ross's view. But, if to say that A is better than B is not to say that it has more of a certain quality, goodness, than B, but only that we ought to adopt a certain attitude towards it, that is, prefer it to B, this explains why a quantitative treatment is not satisfactory.

Another argument in favour of my view is that it explains the fact that goodness is on the face of it a quite different concept from that of any ordinary quality. There is obviously a sense in which one could give a complete description of something without saying whether it was good or bad, which fact shows goodness to be something different from an ordinary quality of the thing which is pronounced good. The naturalist recognises this, but there is another condition which his account does not fulfil. He makes goodness consist in a

relation to certain psychological states, but not a relation of
a kind which we could see to follow necessarily from the
other characteristics of the thing which is good. It does not
follow necessarily from the nature of anything, as far as we
can see, that it will in fact be admired or approved or desired
or pursued by human beings. But the relation in which I hold
goodness to consist, that of being a fitting object of a pro
attitude, can be seen to follow necessarily from the factual
nature of anything that we rightly pronounce to be intrinsically good. If something is a fitting object of a pro attitude
at all, it could not fail to be so without its factual nature being
different from what it is. Yet fittingness is still not itself a part
of its factual nature. The analysis I have accepted thus does
provide a considerable amount of real help in solving philosophical puzzles about ethics.

But many people will remain unsatisfied with a theory like
mine, because instead of explaining our duties by reference
to the good it leaves us with a set of *prima facie* duties for
performing which no reason has been given. They will have
the feeling that the theory gives no real ground why we ought
to do one thing rather than another, while utilitarianism at
least does that. It is important not to state this objection
wrongly. We must not express it by saying that the fact that
something ought to be produced, chosen, approved or pursued,
etc., is not the reason why it is good. For my theory is not
that this constitutes the reason why something is good, but
that this is what is meant by saying that it is good. The reason
why something, A, is good, that is, why we ought to adopt
these attitudes to A, lies in the natural, factual characteristics
of A itself, for instance the characteristic of pleasantness possessed by certain experiences or the characteristic which certain acts have of being the fulfilment of promises. The value
judgements which we see to be true are judgements that,
because of certain natural characteristics which it has, A ought

to be chosen, approved, or pursued. The non-natural, specifically valuational element comes in with the "ought" and only there.

Thus in regard to a particular action that I ought to do there will always be reasons in favour of doing it in the shape of general characteristics which it shares with other actions, for example, the characteristic of fulfilling a contract or that of increasing a neighbour's pleasure. But the objection still has some weight, since I have given no further, more ultimate reason for the general principle that it is fitting to fulfil contracts or to give pleasure to others but just relied on the fact that we see it to be true. It will still be objected that my theory like Ross's does leave the fact that we ought to do one kind of thing rather than another unexplained, while utilitarianism explains it further by reference to the good. True, the utilitarian, if asked to explain why certain things are good-in-themselves, cannot do so, but just has to say that he sees them to be good; but at any rate he does carry the explanation one stage further back. And it does to many seem somehow more rational to take propositions such as "this kind of thing is good" as ultimate and self-vindicating than to hold this view about propositions like "this kind of thing is what I ought to do." It may be objected that I am left with nothing but a chaos of *prima facie* duties for none of which there is any reason beyond themselves, and that I have thus abandoned the essential purpose of Ethics, which is to make coherent our ethical beliefs. It is true that the advantage of utilitarianism relatively to my theory is much less than might appear at first sight, because, unless he is a hedonist, the utilitarian will have to admit an ultimate variety of intrinsic goods, and it might be argued that this is as bad as to admit an ultimate variety of *prima facie* duties. Further, if there are no general rules available for balancing different conflicting *prima facie* duties against each other, neither are there for balancing the different goods and evils of the utilitarian against each other. There is a good deal of force in this reply, but I cannot be satisfied with my position unless it is possible on principle to bring the *prima facie* duties into some kind of system.

Now there are different kinds of system. If we could deduce all ethical duties from a single principle, for example that I ought always to do what I could will everybody else to do, or from one single type of good, for instance pleasure, we should have a system of a certain kind. Such systems in ethics seem to me impracticable. They either give only a pretence of explanation, because they leave outside any concrete idea of the good, which has to be smuggled in unnoticed if the system is to work, or they conflict with moral judgements which we see to be true. They do not do justice to the complexity of ethics or of life.

But you may have a system of another kind. The systematic character of a body of beliefs may lie not in the fact that they are all deducible from one and the same principle but in the fact that, although no one of the beliefs can occupy the exalted position of being premise for all the rest, they are all logically related to each other so that you could not alter any one without contradicting others. It is a system of this sort that is envisaged in the coherence theory of truth. Could the true propositions of ethics form a system of this kind? Clearly not in the full sense. For one could certainly deny some true ethical propositions without logically contradicting any others. But there is still, I think, a sense in which they may be said to form a system. They form a system in the sense that the different ultimate *prima facie* duties are so connected that to fulfil any one harmonizes with and forwards in general and on principle the fulfilment of others. The utilitarians hold that it is generally a duty to tell the truth, keep promises, be just, make reparation for wrong one has done, treat our parents with love, etc.; but, as is well known, they maintain that what makes these kinds of action duties is that they further other goods. The view that this is the only reason for their being duties has been challenged by non-utilitarians, but hardly the view that they do further other goods and on the whole make for the best state of society attainable all round. Now "further other goods" becomes on the view I have suggested "further what ought, other things being equal, to be furthered on its own account," that is, fulfil other *prima facie* duties. But if the different *prima facie* duties play into each others' hands in this way, that may well serve as a confirmation that we are on the right lines in admitting them, so that we are not wholly dependent on intuition, but have also this "coherence" test.

But what about the undoubted clashes that do occur at times between different *prima facie* duties? Surely I may easily be placed in a situation in which I have to break one of two promises because the two are incompatible with each other, or to neglect either my *prima facie* duty to a relative or my *prima facie* duty to the state? Is not this sufficient to show that the line of argument suggested is a *cul-de-sac*, and that the *prima facie* duties cannot possibly be regarded as constituting a system?

It may be retorted, however, that, if we investigate such clashes, we find that, so far from refuting, they support the view that the *prima facie* duties constitute a system in some sense like the one I suggested. Let us take one of the acutest possible clashes, that arising in the case of war. Suppose one's country has promised to help another country against aggression and that country is wrongfully attacked by a Power whose mode of government we cannot help regarding as a tyranny which has deliberately and persistently set aside in theory and practice principles of justice and liberty that we consider quite fundamental to civilisation. What are we to do? If we fight, we are certainly violating *prima facie* duties by the killing and other evil practices which war involves. If we do not fight, we are breaking our solemn word and letting a higher form of civilisation be overthrown by a lower and injustice and wrong triumph over right. Whichever answer we give, it is quite clear that we shall be violating some *prima facie* duties. But this does not disprove the view that the *prima facie* duties constitute a system. On the contrary it supports it. For why does this acute clash arise? Only because somebody has done wrong first. In every war at least one party is to blame. But, if the *prima facie* duties do constitute a system, surely the only thing to expect is that, if you violate one, you or someone else will tend to be brought into a position in which others have to be violated. To take an analogy, nobody would put forward as an objection to the systematic or coherent character of arithmetic that, if you start by believing that two plus two equals five or five plus seven equals eleven, or (without believing these propositions) wilfully proceed in your calculations as if they were true you will arrive at a host of other false propositions by arguing consistently from your premises. This will happen just because the different arithmetical propositions do constitute a system in which they all hang together.

Similarly the occurrence of clashes as a result of violating one *prima facie* duty is not a contradiction but a confirmation of the view that the *prima facie* duties constitute a system. If they do constitute a system, clashes are just what one ought to expect under these circumstances; and most of the serious clashes which occur in fact are due to previous violations of duty on the part of some person, or at least to mistakes as to what was his duty. If I make two inconsistent promises I must break one, but then I have already, intentionally or unintentionally, acted wrongly in making them. Again I may have to choose between lying and exposing to punishment as a criminal a person whom I love, but then either he has already done wrong in committing a crime or the government or administration has done wrong in treating as a crime the kind of act he has done. A man lives under a social system such that he cannot give satisfactory opportunities to his family without grasping after material gain somewhat more zealously than is desirable; that is because the social system is morally evil in so far as, through being too competitive, it encourages selfishness and makes money too much the standard of success. One cannot rapidly overthrow an existing bad political or economic system in some country without a violent revolution which will involve great misery and injustice; but that clash arises because the people who think they benefit by it are too much concerned for their own interests and too little for the welfare of others to let it be amended peaceably, and perhaps because the people who lose by it are too bitter and not disciplined enough to avoid revolutionary excesses. We must not indeed go too far on these lines. All clashes cannot be explained in this way. Natural disasters, as well as wars and bad social systems, may cause grave clashes; for example there is the well known case of lying in order to save some invalid from hearing bad news, or again a man might through an earthquake be placed in a position in which he had to choose between saving the life of his child and the lives of two other persons unknown to him. So the most we can say is that in general and on principle the *prima facie* duties fit together, that to fulfil one tends, of its intrinsic nature, to fulfil others, and to violate one tends to the violation of others. But this much we can say, and this helps to confirm the belief that any one of them is a genuine *prima facie* duty.

We need not therefore confine ourselves to saying that the ultimate *prima facie* duties are known intuitively; we can add that our intuitions of them are confirmed by the fact that to further one on the whole furthers others and to violate one tends to involve sooner or later violating others. There is thus a kind of coherence test available after all to supplement intuition. To this it may be objected that to see something to be an ultimate *prima facie* duty is to see that it ought to be done on its own account, and that the fact that to do it will have the effect of facilitating the fulfilment of other *prima facie duties* is therefore quite irrelevant to the question whether it is an ultimate *prima facie* duty or not. It is relevant to the question whether it ought to be done, but not to the question whether it ought to be done on its own account, and the latter is the question we are asking when we ask whether it is an ultimate *prima facie* duty, for instance, to keep promises or not. Obviously we cannot show that we ought to keep promises just because we have made them by showing that there are other good reasons for keeping them.

But the different goods are more closely connected with each other than this objection assumes. To recognise that we have a *prima facie* duty to keep promises is to recognise that keeping promises is intrinsically good; but to say this is not to say that keeping promises would be good altogether apart from its relations to anything else. When we say that something is good-in-itself we certainly mean that it really has the property of goodness itself and not only that its effects have it. We mean that it is to be valued for itself and not merely as a means to something else, but it does not follow that it would have this property in a quite different context. This, it seems to me, would not necessarily follow even if good were a quality; [9] *a fortiori* it does not follow if to call something good just means that it is fitting that we should have a certain attitude towards it. Consequently the fact that something which we seem to see intuitively to be intrinsically good is linked up with other goods may still help to provide a confirmation of our intuitive belief that it is intrinsically good. This would

---

[9] V. above, p. 114.

be the case to some extent even if the connection were only one of cause and effect, for we must expect good on principle and *per se* to produce good rather than evil and *vice versa*. No doubt good can be wrung out of evil but only by conquering it, for instance by bearing it well, and in that case the cause of the good gained does not lie wholly in the evil. Fresh good is produced by the furtherance of good and the conquering of evil.

But the connection between the different goods is closer than these remarks about causation suggest. It is not only that, for example, the keeping of promises is a cause which produces good effects. It can be seen to be linked up with the other kinds of good in respect of its essential nature and not merely by causal laws. In the first place, it follows necessarily that a person who has a fitting regard for the intrinsic value of true cognition will be averse to thus deceiving people. In the second place, it follows from any real sense of regard for the well-being of others that we shall not wish to cheat and disappoint them by breaking our promises, promise-keeping is bound up necessarily with the good of benevolence or love. In the third place, there would be no point in keeping a promise if it did not give any satisfaction at all to anybody, even the promisee. It is therefore bound up with hedonistic good. Fourthly, it is unfair to benefit by the promises of others, as we cannot help doing, and yet not keep our own, an argument which links promise-keeping with the good of justice. If you ask me whether promise-keeping would still be a good if it did not stand in any of these relations I could not say that it would, or rather I should answer that the question is absurd. It would not then be promise-keeping at all. It does not follow that we ought absolutely without exception to keep promises, for what follows from the nature of promise-keeping is that it has a general inherent tendency to be associated with these goods, not that this tendency is in all cases realised more strongly by keeping than by breaking a particular promise. It may happen that an action which is an example of promise-keeping has other characteristics which are not of such a desirable nature, for instance I may have promised to commit a murder. If in a particular case to break a promise is really for the good of the promisee, it may be more in accord with benevolence to break it than to keep it and more in accord with hedonistic good.

Now, if we had an ostensible intuition of the goodness of promise-keeping and not of the goodness of true cognition, benevolence and fairness, our intuitive conviction that promise-keeping is good (a *prima facie* duty) would be in a less strong position than is the case as things are, for now it is also supported by the ostensible intuitions that each of these other things is good. If any of them are intrinsically good; promise-keeping is in so far good and should in so far be pursued on its own account. For I am not merely saying that promise-keeping is good as a means for producing certain effects. The attitude to truth, to other persons, to the general happiness, and to the requirements of reciprocal justice, involved in promise-keeping is such that it must be better *per se* than promise-breaking if a right attitude to any of the above-mentioned itself has intrinsic value. So we now have not just one ostensible intuition, but a number of such intuitions confirming each other. That something like this confirmation, perhaps not always so complete, can be given of all genuine *prima facie* duties seems to me likely. It is significant how often the same action may be rightly recommended on different grounds, and this fact, which incidentally has made a multitude of conflicting ethical theories possible, shows the fundamental coherence of different *prima facie* duties. Benevolence can itself be commended on grounds of justice because it is unfair to expect kindness from others in case of need and yet not be prepared to give it when others are in need. All or most of the other *prima facie* duties may indeed be commended on the ground that they are bound up with the duty of promise-keeping; that is, they must be fulfilled if we are to keep faith with the community by fulfilling reasonable expectations, including the expectation that members of a community will sometimes devote themselves to the benefit of the community in ways the particular character of which cannot from the nature of the case be foreseen by others. But this is not to say that all other duties should be deduced from the duty of promise-keeping as their ultimate *raison d'être*. The different *prima facie* duties may confirm each other without any one being supreme. Similarly the goods of intellectual, aesthetic, and moral development are not just alien and indifferent to each other. They may accidentally clash, but this will be either because a man has not time to develop all sides of his nature as much as he would like or because the development of one side may become more or less warped and perverse. It is generally realised on the contrary that each side of human nature has something to give to the others, and that they cannot be sharply separated from each other. Thus artists who have written on the purpose of their art generally claim to be not merely creating beauty but conveying some kind of truth and thus benefiting also the intellectual side of man as well as cultivating and ennobling the emotions and making men more sensitive to the good. It is the belief of thinkers, defended in this book by the very emphasis I am giving to the coherence test, that thought can help the ethical side of our nature, and the intellectual quality of rationality and consistency is essentially connected with at least such a virtue as justice. In other quarters emphasis has been rightly laid on a certain aesthetic quality possessed by coherent theories and well rounded arguments and on the effect on one's emotional and aesthetic sides of the disinterested contemplation of truth whether in science or philosophy. There is essentially an aesthetic and moral quality about good intellectual development, an intellectual and moral quality about good aesthetic development and an aesthetic and intellectual quality about good moral development. To work out in full these suggestions towards a coherent theory of ethics would be to carry me far beyond the scope of this book, but what I have said at any rate shows that I am not necessarily reduced to a mere chaos of unrelated and unconfirmable *prima facie* duties.

Some thinkers have stressed intuition and some coherence, but both are needed in ethics. The coherence test plays an essential part in confirming, amending, clarifying and extending what first presents itself as a more or less confused intuition. Thus it is by the use of the coherence test that humanity passes —alas how slowly!—from moral principles almost confined to dealings with other members of the agent's small tribal group to a really universal application of these principles, since men gradually come to recognize that the limits imposed by themselves on the classes of those towards whom they have duties of benevolence and justice are arbitrary and inconsistent. On the other hand without ethical intuition there would be no material to which the coherence test could be applied. Similarly, we need both intuition and inference not only for the establishment and justification of general principles but in order to make adequate moral decisions in particular cases.[10] In emphasising coherence I do not indeed mean to imply that intellectual consistency is of chief value in ethics. It is very important as a help to finding what is right, but practical ethics does not lie merely in finding out what is right, it lies in the often much more difficult and much less pleasant task of doing what is right. Further, even for the purpose of find-

---

[10] For the part played by inference here and the different modes of inference used v. my book on *The Morality of Punishment with Some Suggestions for a General Theory of Ethics.* (Kegan Paul, London, 1929), pp. 195–215.

ing out what is right, empirical knowledge of the likely consequences is another factor which cannot be supplied by the
philosopher as such and is yet of the extremest importance.

This book has been a discussion of what good is, not of what
things are good, and it is therefore neither an attempt to commend certain values (good things) nor to give advice on the
solution of concrete ethical problems.   It is a doubtful point
how much the philosopher can do in either direction, though
he can do something, but anything he does will not be a direct
deduction from the analysis of good.   Still less could I be
expected by such a deduction to persuade people to do what
they know to be their duty, but in any case this is the task
not of the philosopher but of the preacher. But this is not to
say that I think my book of no practical value. I think that
it is an extremely important task, both practically and theoretically, to stem the tide of subjectivism and naturalism in
ethics, for the development of such beliefs seems to me bound
to weaken seriously the sense of moral obligation by taking
away any rational basis for ethics. To stem this tide we need
three things—criticism of the subjectivists and naturalists,
reply to their criticisms, and a positive opposing theory as to
what good is. These I have tried to supply; and if I have at
all succeeded it seems to me that I have done something of
practical as well as theoretical importance, though a philosopher must be careful to avoid the error of overestimating the
effects on practice of his theories.

Index

Admiration, 154 ff., 157-58, 173, 180 n.
Aesthetic value, 164, 173, 211.
Analysis in philosophy, 31-2, 37-8, 43 ff., 49. See Definition.
Anti attitude, 168.
Approval, as basis of definition of good, and ought, 4 ff., 58 ff., 100 ff., 154 ff., 177.
Argument, in ethics, 5, 30, 34. See Coherence test.
Aristotle, 34.

Bad, different senses of, 117; definition of, 167-68.
Biological definitions of ethical concepts, 41, 73-4.
Bosanquet, B., 80 n.
Bradley, F. H., 80 n.
Brandt, Prof. R. B., 25.
Broad, Prof. C. D., 11, 23, 40 ff., 73 n., 100 ff. 118 n., 132.
Butler, Bishop, 57-8.

Carritt, E. F., 11 n., 112 n.
Children, ethical development in, 23-4, 56, 182-83.
Class-relation, definition of good in terms of, 104-6, 117.
Coherence theory of ethics, 13, 79-101; coherence test, 203-12.
Commands, theory reducing ethical judgements to, 10, 13-17, 56-7, 75-6. 106 ff.
Commonsense, 31-2, 54-5.
Consequences, in ethics, 19, 21, 118 ff., 125-26, 187 ff.
Cruelty, 64, 163-64, 165.

Definition, general nature of, 41 ff., 46-8, 78-9, 99-100; final definition of good, 146 ff.; the indefinable, 45 ff., 78, 83, 146-47, 178.

Descriptive theory of good, 100 ff.
Desire, as basis of definition of good, 17-18, 62-70, 97-8, 101 ff., 166; as motive for action, 51-2, 137 ff.
Determinism, 135.
Differences of belief in ethics, 18-22, 25 ff., 120-21.
Disapproval. See Approval.
Duty, meaning of term, 123-25, 170-71; sense of duty as motive, 141 ff. See Moral obligation.

Education, ethical, 182-83.
Efficient, 113.
Egoism, 18, 50, 111.
Emotion, connection with ethics, 4 ff., 12-13, 24 ff., 56 ff., 76, 101 ff., 151, 164 ff., 178 ff., 182-83.
Empiricism, in ethics, 38 ff., 44, 51-3.
End, as opposed to means. See Intrinsic goodness.
Evil, 117, 208.
Evolution, 73-4, 105-6.
Exclamations, theory reducing "ethical judgements" to, 10 ff.
Experience, relevance to ethics of, 20, 38 ff., 49-51, 52-3.

Feeling, 2 ff. See Emotion.
Field, Prof. G. C., 51.
Fittingness, 132-33, 135-36, 150 ff., 156-58, 169-73, 176 ff., 184-85, 189 ff., 201.
Function, definition of good in terms of, 105-6.

God, 106-11, 123, 134-35, 170.
Greatest good, 188 ff.

Harmony, 81, 98-9.
Hedonism, 50, 186. See Utilitarianism.
Hume, David, 41, 52, 88, 165.
Hypothetical imperatives, 135, 177 n.

213